Contents

Part I:
DOCUMENTS ON THE
ANNIVERSARY OF THE HOLOCAUST

Part II:
1998 VATICAN STATEMENT AND COMMENTARIES

Introduction

Archbishop Alexander J. Brunett
Chair, Bishops' Committee for Ecumenical and Interreligious Affairs
National Conference of Catholic Bishops, U.S.A.

T his is "the century of the *Shoah*," as Pope John Paul II has called it. He sees the massive cataclysm of the Holocaust as something more than yet another historical atrocity, and the preservation of its memory as something to which the faithful of the Church are called, alongside the Jewish people. Addressing Jewish leaders in Warsaw, he said, "Today the people of Israel, perhaps more than ever before, finds itself at the center of the attention of the nations of the world, above all because of this terrible experience, through which you have become a warning voice for all humanity, for all nations, all the powers of the world, all systems and every person. More than anyone else, it is precisely you who have become this saving warning. I think that in this sense you continue your particular vocation, showing yourselves to be still heirs of that election to which God is faithful. This is your mission in the contemporary world before the peoples, the nations, all of humanity, the Church. And in this Church all peoples and nations feel united to you in this mission" (June 14, 1987).[1]

The statements collected here represent the attempts of the national hierarchies of many of the nations most deeply involved in the events of the *Shoah* to grapple with the immense complexities of the histories of their own nations and local churches a half century ago. The Holy See's "We Remember: A Reflection on the *Shoah*" is an effort to engage the whole Church in the examination of conscience called for by Pope John Paul II in *Tertio Millennio Adveniente (On the Coming of the Third Millennium)*.

We believe that these texts should be known and studied by Catholics even in local communities where few Jews reside and in those which were not directly involved in World War II. The reasons given by "We Remember" (section V) are threefold:

1. There exists a close spiritual bond of faith which links Christians to the Jews.
2. Many Christians were involved in the events of this catastrophe, some as fellow victims, some as rescuers, but too many others sadly as bystanders or perpetrators. As Christians we are all linked together in the Church, not only with the goodness of saints but also with the failures of sinners.
3. One cannot overstate the abiding need to preserve the memory of the event itself as a warning for future generations.

Sometimes our people ask whether the preservation of this memory pertains more to the Jewish people than to us since it is they who saw so many millions of their family members perish. Surely it must be realized that the death of these millions touches first of all the Jews with an immediacy that is specifically theirs. But the death of those who were taken represents a loss not only to their families, grave as that is, but a loss to the world that is incalculable. That alone is reason enough for all to mourn and to remember.

Still there is a further compelling need to do so. In writing to the American bishops, John Hotchkin, their director of ecumenical and interreligious affairs, took this up. He observed that the chillingly systematic effort to exterminate an entire people, not for what they had done nor for any threat they posed, but simply for being who they were—whether young or old; every last man, woman, and child—is an attempt at evil on a nearly unimaginable scale. Thus the *Shoah* raises in a most awful way the darkest questions the mystery of evil has put to the human family in our time. We may never get to the bottom of these questions. For something this evil there is in the end no explanation the mind can accept. It remains a dark and threatening mystery. But what we cannot explain, we must nevertheless remember. The warning contained in the memory is our best common shield and defense. The evil that turns humanity against humanity, cheapening its life, degrading it, bent on its destruction, still lurks in the world. It does not rest and neither must we in our remembering, for it is by remembering the unspeakable horror that did in fact happen that we remain awake and alert to the possibility that what happened could be attempted again. It is through our common remembrance of those who perished that they shield the living.

This is a cataclysm unlike any other in human history. Indeed, the theologian David Tracy has written of it as an "interruption" of history, an event in which "our history crashes against itself." It is as if time stopped, and history thereafter could never again be the same. For this reason it is imperative that the memory be kept and the story be told from generation to generation. The texts assembled here are intended for that purpose. They have been gathered together in this volume so they may more readily be studied and shared.

Note
1. Papal texts cited in this volume up to 1995 can be found in E. Fisher and L. Klenicki, eds., *Spiritual Pilgrimage: Pope John Paul II on Jews and Judaism, 1979-1995* (New York: Crossroad, 1995), arranged in chronological order. More recent texts can be found in Origins.

Part I:
DOCUMENTS ON THE ANNIVERSARY OF THE HOLOCAUST

Joint Statement on the Occasion of the Fiftieth Anniversary of the Holocaust

Hungarian Bishops and Ecumenical Council of Churches in Hungary
November 1994

The bishops of the Hungarian Catholic Church as well as the bishops and leading pastors of the member churches of the Ecumenical Council of Churches in Hungary and the communities they are here representing commemorate in piety the tragic events of fifty years ago, when Jews living in Hungary were dragged off to concentration camps and slaughtered in cold blood. We consider it as the greatest shame of our twentieth century that hundreds of thousands of lives were extinguished merely because of their origin.

On the anniversary of these painful events we pay the tribute of respect to the memory of the victims. Conforming to the message of the Scripture we all consider the Holocaust as an unpardonable sin. This crime burdens our history as well as our communities and reminds us of the obligation of propitiation, apart from pious commemoration.

On the occasion of the anniversary we have to state that not only the perpetrators of this insane crime are responsible for it but all those who, although they declared themselves members of our churches, through fear, cowardice, or opportunism, failed to raise their voices against the mass humiliation, deportation, and murder of their Jewish neighbors. Before God we now ask forgiveness for this failure committed in the time of disaster fifty years ago.

We look at those, who in that dehumanized age, rescued lives at the cost of their own, or endangering it, and surmounting denominational considerations, protested with universal and general effect against the diabolical plots.

It is a task of conscience for us all to strengthen the service of reconciliation in our communities, for this is the only way for all persons to be equally respected and live in mutual understanding and love.

We have to aim at developing true humaneness, so that there will be no more antisemitism or any kind of discrimination, and so that the crimes of the past will never happen again.

Opportunity to Re-examine Relationships with the Jews

German Bishops
January 1995

On January 27, 1945, the concentration camps of Auschwitz and Auschwitz-Birkenau were liberated. Numerous people were murdered there in a terrible manner: Poles, Russians, Rom and Sinti people (Gypsies), as well as members of other nations. The overwhelming majority of prisoners and victims in this camp consisted of Jews. Therefore Auschwitz has become the symbol of the extermination of European Jewry, which is called *Holocaust* or—using the Hebrew term—*Shoah.*

The crime against the Jews was planned and put into action by the National Socialist rulers in Germany. The "unprecedented crime" which was the *Shoah* (Pope John Paul II, address to the Jewish leaders of Poland, June 9, 1991) still raises many questions which we must not evade. The commemoration of the fiftieth anniversary of the liberation of Auschwitz gives German Catholics the opportunity to re-examine their relationship with the Jews.

At the same time this day recalls the fact that Auschwitz is also part of the Polish history of suffering and burdens the relationship between Poles and Germans.

Already during earlier centuries, Jews were exposed to persecution, oppression, expulsion, and even to mortal danger. Many looked for and found refuge in Poland. However, there were also places and regions in Germany where Jews could live relatively untroubled. Since the eighteenth century, there was a new chance of a peaceful coexistence in Germany. Jews decisively contributed toward the development of German science and culture. Nevertheless, an anti-Jewish attitude remained, also within the Church.

This was one of the reasons why, during the years of the Third Reich, Christians did not offer due resistance to racial antisemitism. Many times there was failure and guilt among Catholics. Not a few of them got involved in the ideology of National Socialism and remained unmoved in the face of the crimes committed against Jewish-owned property and the life of the Jews. Others paved the way for crimes or even became criminals themselves.

It is unknown how many people were horrified at the disappearance of their Jewish neighbors and yet were not strong enough to raise their voices in protest. Those who rendered aid to others, thereby risking their own lives, frequently did not receive support.

Today the fact is weighing heavily on our minds that there were but individual initiatives to help persecuted Jews and that even the pogroms of November 1938 were not followed by public and express protest—i.e., when hundreds of synagogues were set on fire and vandalized, cemeteries were desecrated, thousands of Jewish-owned shops were demolished, innumerable dwellings of Jewish families were damaged and looted, people were ridiculed, ill-treated, and even killed.

The retrospect on the events of November 1938 and on the terror regime of the National Socialists during twelve years visualizes the heavy burden of history. It recalls "that the Church, which we proclaim as holy and which we honor as a mystery, is also a sinful Church and in need of conversion" (statement by the German and Austrian bishops conferences on the fiftieth anniversary of the November 1938 pogroms).

The failure and guilt of that time have also a church dimension. We are reminded of that fact when quoting the witness given by the joint synod of dioceses in the Federal Republic of Germany:

> We are that country whose recent political history was darkened
> by the attempt to systematically exterminate the Jewish people.
> And in this period of National Socialism—despite the exemplary

behavior of some individuals and groups—we were nevertheless, as a whole, a church community who kept on living our lives while turning our backs too often on the fate of this persecuted Jewish people. We looked too fixedly at the threat to our own institutions and remained silent about the crimes committed against the Jews and Judaism. . . . The practical sincerity of our will of renewal is also linked to the confession of this guilt and the willingness to painfully learn from this history of guilt of our country and of our church as well. ("Our Hope," resolution of November 22, 1975)

We request the Jewish people to hear this word of conversion and will of renewal.

Auschwitz faces us Christians with the question of what relationship we have with the Jews and whether this relationship corresponds to the spirit of Jesus Christ. Antisemitism is "a sin against God and humanity," as Pope John Paul II has said many times. In the Church there must not be any room for or consent to hostility toward Jews. Christians must not harbor aversion, dislike, and, even less, feelings of hatred for Jews and Judaism. Wherever such an attitude comes to light, they have the duty to offer public and express resistance.

The Church respects the autonomy of Judaism. Simultaneously she has to learn anew that she is descended from Israel and remains linked to its patrimony concerning faith, ethos, and liturgy. Wherever it is possible, Christian and Jewish communities should cultivate mutual contacts. We have to do everything in our power to enable Jews and Christians in our country to live together as good neighbors. In this way they will make their own distinctive contribution to a Europe whose past was darkened by the *Shoah* and which, in the future, is to become a continent of solidarity.

The Victims of Nazi Ideology

Polish Bishops
January 1995

Half a century has passed since the liberation of the Auschwitz-Birkenau concentration camp on January 27, 1945. Once again our attention is drawn to the painful reality and symbolism of this camp, where more than 1 million Jews, Poles (70,000-75,000), Gypsies (21,000), Russians (15,000), and other nationalities (10,000-15,000) found an atrocious death.

Only a few months into the war, in the spring of 1940, the Nazi Germans created the Auschwitz concentration camp on occupied Polish territory annexed to the Third Reich. At the beginning of its existence, the first prisoners and victims were thousands of Poles, mainly intelligentsia, members of the resistance movement as well as clergy and people representing almost all walks of life. There probably isn't a Polish family that hasn't lost someone close at Auschwitz or at another camp. With great respect we bow our heads before the infinite suffering which was often accepted in a deep Christian spirit. An eloquent example is the heroic figure of Fr. Maximilian Kolbe, who sacrificed his life for a fellow prisoner in August 1941. He was beatified by Pope Paul VI and canonized by Pope John Paul II. His victory, motivated by the Gospel of Jesus Christ, bears witness to the power of love and goodness in a world of outrage and violence.

Almost from the beginning, Polish Jews were sent to this camp, as part of Polish society, to be destroyed. Since 1942, the Auschwitz-Birkenau complex, as well as other camps in occupied Poland, as a result of the Wannsee Conference became extermination camps to realize the criminal ideology of the "final solution," in other words, the plan to murder all European Jews. The Nazis transported to the death camps Jews from all European countries occupied by Hitler. Not only Auschwitz, but also Majdanek, Treblinka, Belzec, Chelmno, and others were located in occupied Poland by the Germans as places to exterminate Jews, because this was where the majority of European Jews lived and, therefore, such a Nazi crime could be better hidden from world public opinion in a country totally occupied and even partly annexed to the Third Reich.

It is estimated today that more than 1 million Jews died at Auschwitz-Birkenau alone. Consequently, even though members of other nations also perished at this camp, nevertheless, Jews consider this camp a symbol of the total extermination of their nation. "The very people who received from God the commandment 'Thou shalt not kill,' itself experienced in a particular way what is meant by killing" (John Paul II, homily at Auschwitz-Birkenau death camp, June 7, 1979).

Extermination, called *Shoah*, has weighed painfully not only in relations between Germans and Jews, but also to a great extent in relations between Jews and Poles, who together, though not to the same degree, were the victims of Nazi ideology. Because they lived in close proximity, they became involuntary witnesses to the extermination of Jews. Regretfully, it has to be stated that for many years Auschwitz-Birkenau was treated by the communist regime almost entirely in terms of an anti-fascist struggle that did not help to convey the extent of the extermination of Jews.

It must be underlined that Poles and Jews have lived in this country for centuries, and although now and again conflicts did arise, they considered it their homeland. Driven out of western Europe, Jews found refuge in Poland. Consequently, Poland often had the reputation of being *paradisus Judaerorum* ("a Jewish paradise"), because here they could live according to their customs, religion, and culture. Contrary to many European countries, until the time of World War II, Jews were never driven out of Poland. About 80 percent of Jews living in the world today can trace their descent through their parents and/or grandparents to roots in Poland.

The loss of Polish independence and Poland's partition by Russia, Austria, and Prussia—which lasted more than 120 years—brought about, in the midst of other dramatic consequences, a deterioration in Polish-Jewish relations. In the period of time between World War I and World War II, when Poland, after regaining her independence in 1918, sought to find forms of her own identity, new conflicts arose. Their underlying factors were of psychological, economic, political and religious nature but never racist. Despite the antisemitism of some circles, shortly before the outbreak of World War II, when Hitler's repressions intensified, it was Poland that accepted thousands of Jews from Germany.

Seeing the Nazi extermination of Jews, many Poles reacted with heroic courage and sacrifice, risking their lives and that of their families. The virtues of the Gospel and solidarity with the suffering and the persecuted motivated almost every convent in the general government to give Jewish children refuge. Many Poles lost their lives, in defiance of threats of the death penalty with regard to themselves and their family members, because they dared to shelter Jews. It should be mentioned that, as a consequence of giving refuge to Jews, the rule of common responsibility was applied to Poles. Often whole families, from children to grandparents, were killed for harboring Jews. In acknowledgment of this, thousands were awarded with medals "righteous among the nations of the world." Nameless others also brought help.

Unfortunately, there were also those who were capable of actions unworthy of being called Christian. There were those who not only blackmailed, but also gave away Jews in hiding into German hands. Nothing can justify such an attitude, though the inhumane time of war and the cruelty of the Nazis led to Jews, themselves tormented by the occupier, being forced to hand over their brothers into the hands of the Germans. Once again, we recall the words of the Polish bishops' pastoral letter that was read at all Catholic churches and chapels on January 20, 1991, which stated: "In spite of numerous heroic examples of Polish Christians, there were those who remained indifferent to that inconceivable tragedy. In particular, we mourn the fact that there were also those among Catholics who in some way had contributed to the death of Jews. They will forever remain a source of remorse in the social dimension."

The creators of Auschwitz were the Nazi Germans, not Poles. Everything that symbolizes this death camp is a result of a National Socialist ideology that was not born in Poland. Another totalitarian system, similar to the Nazi, which was communism, gathered many millions in a harvest of death. Nazism also meant trampling on the dignity of the human being as an image of God. There existed a dramatic community of fate between Poles and Jews in constraint and ruthless extermination. However, it was the Jews who became the victims of the Nazi plan of systematic and total liquidation. "An insane ideology decided on this plan in the name of a wretched form of racism and carried it out mercilessly" (John Paul II, beatification of Edith Stein, Cologne, Germany, May 1, 1987).

The world in which the cruelties of Auschwitz were carried out was also a world redeemed and at the same time a world of challenge, even after the *Shoah,* from where arises the message to all Christians that they should reveal God in their actions and not contribute to the questioning of his presence. God was and continues to be everywhere. What is satanic and represents hatred never originates from God but from man, who submits himself to the influence of the Evil One and doesn't respect the dignity of the human being or God's commandments.

The half century that has passed since the liberation of Auschwitz-Birkenau obliges us to express a clear objection to all signs of disregard for human dignity such as racism, antisemitism, xenophobia, and anti-Polish attitudes. Living in a country marked with the burden of a horrible event called *Shoah,* with Edith Stein, who died at Auschwitz because she was a Jew, with faith and total confidence in God, the Father of all humanity, we emphatically repeat: Hatred will never have the last word in this world (John Paul II's message prior to visiting the Federal Republic of Germany, April 25, 1987).

The only guarantee of this is to educate future generations in the spirit of mutual respect, tolerance, and love according to the recommendations contained in the Holy See's *Notes on the Correct Way to Present the Jews and Judaism in Preaching and Catechesis in the Catholic Church* (June 24, 1985).

Commemorating the Liberation of Auschwitz

Archbishop Oscar Lipscomb
Chair, U.S. Bishops' Committee on Ecumenical and Interreligious Affairs
January 1995

The year 1995 marks the fiftieth anniversary of the end of the Second World War. Both the Atlantic and the Pacific communities of nations will be commemorating the decisive events of the closing of the most violent and murderous war in human history. On May 8, 1945, Nazi Germany finally admitted its defeat. On September 2, 1945, Japan also surrendered unconditionally. But the remembrances of the victories of the Allies at such tremendous cost in human lives must not mask the evils perpetrated during the war itself and the moral lessons still to be learned by the human community from those terrible events.

So it is most fitting that the first major anniversary of the year to be commemorated is the liberation on January 27, 1945, by Soviet troops of the infamous death camp of Auschwitz-Birkenau, the name of which has come to symbolize in our collective memory the worst evils of which humanity has shown itself capable. Pope John Paul II, who lived through that period in his native Poland, has called this "the century of the *Shoah* [Holocaust]."

Although the full nature of the horrors of the Nazi death camps was not revealed until the liberation of the camps throughout occupied Europe by the Allied forces, those who fought the war did have a real sense of what was at stake in the struggle against Nazism and did raise their voices in strong moral protest. On November 14, 1942, while the systematic genocide of the Jewish people was at its most intense, the National Catholic Welfare Conference "in the name of the bishops of the United States," declared:

> Our country has been forced into the most devastating war of all time. This war . . . involves unquestionably the most important moral issue of today. Some nations are united in waging war to bring about a slave world—a world that would deprive man of his divinely conferred dignity, reject human freedom, and permit no religious liberty. . . .
>
> Since the murderous assault on Poland, utterly devoid of any semblance of humanity, there has been a premeditated and systematic extermination of the people of this nation. The same satanic technique is being applied to many other peoples. We feel a deep sense of revulsion against the cruel indignities heaped upon the Jews in conquered countries and upon defenseless peoples not of our faith.
>
> We join with our brother bishops in subjugated France in a statement attributed to them: "Deeply moved by the mass arrests and maltreatment of Jews, we cannot stifle the cry of our conscience. In the name of humanity and Christian principles our voice is raised in favor of imprescriptible rights of human nature." We raise our voice in protest against despotic tyrants who have lost all sense of humanity by condemning thousands of innocent persons to death in subjugated countries as acts of reprisal [and] by placing thousands of innocent victims in concentration camps.

The context of this statement was the line of papal condemnations of anti-semitism and Nazism beginning with Pope Pius XI's famous dictum that all Christians, as children of Abraham, are themselves "spiritual Semites." In 1937, Pius XI issued a German-language encyclical which had to be smuggled into the Third Reich to be read in all pulpits. This stern encyclical, *Mit Brennender Sorge (With Burning Sorrow)*, condemned the "racialism" of Nazi ideology as wholly opposed to essential Catholic doctrine and condemned Nazism as a form of pagan idolatry.

Pope Pius XII maintained this teaching of his predecessor throughout his pontificate. In his Christmas message of 1942, he pleaded for "the hundreds of thousands who, through no fault of their own, only because of their nationality or descent, are condemned to death." Observers at the time, including the editorial of *The New York Times* for December 25, 1942, understood this as a reference to the plight of the Jews. The American, French, and other bishops of the world who joined the condemnations of Nazi genocide believed themselves to be following the lead of the Holy Father.

As we join this year with our fellow Americans, especially our Jewish sisters and brothers, in prayerful commemorations of the millions of victims of the Holocaust, American Catholics will recall with profound gratitude the tremendous sacrifices made by the generation which defeated Hitler. But, as Americans and as Catholics, we also recall with humility and a sense of regret the opportunities that were lost to save lives. We recall the rejection by our government of the pleas from Jewish leaders to bomb the railroad lines leading to Auschwitz—a rejection that came at the very time that U.S. bombers were flying over the camp on their way to other targets!

We remember, too, the bitter enforcement of the draconian immigration laws of the period, restrictions which kept this country from becoming the asylum for Jews, Catholics, and others that it should have been and should now be. This is symbolized for us in the refusal of American authorities to allow the ship, the *St. Louis*, to disembark several hundred Jewish refugees as it sat in New York harbor within sight of the Statue of Liberty. Returned to Europe, most of these helpless men, women, and children were soon lost in the death camps. Today we see again bitter debates over immigration policy, including efforts to exclude persons who are undocumented—including children—from access to critical services such as health care and education. May our reflections on the tragedy of the passengers of the *St. Louis* help to bring about a generous response to immigrants seeking to contribute to this society.

Having fought the war against Hitler, Americans do not feel personal guilt for what the Nazis did. But American Christians do acknowledge a real sense of responsibility for what fellow members in the community of the baptized did not do to save lives. We take to heart the call to us of Pope John Paul II that all Catholics, as the turn of the millennium draws near, undertake an examination of conscience. "The Church . . . cannot cross the threshold of the new millennium without encouraging her children to purify themselves, through repentance, of past errors and instances of infidelity, inconsistency, and slowness to act" *(Tertio Millennio Adveniente,* no. 33).

In our examination also, we honor the memory of our fellow Catholics of the time, those who were themselves victims of Nazism and those who did speak out and act to save Jewish lives: women such as the Sisters of Sion, who at great risk to their own lives hid hundreds of Jews in their convents throughout occupied Europe, and men such as Jan Karski, who as a representative of the Polish government in exile smuggled himself into the Warsaw ghetto and a concentration camp in order to bring to the Allied governments firsthand awareness of what was going on, and Archbishops Angelo Roncalli (later Pope John XXIII) and Angelo Rotta, who as nuncios appointed by Pope Pius XII in Turkey and Hungary, respectively, were responsible for saving thousands of Jewish lives. We remember such figures with profound humility, since we know that such "angels of mercy" were far too few and since we do not know with certainty what we might do in similar dire circumstances. But it is they who should be educational models in the formation of our Catholic children today.

Our spirit in remembering the fiftieth anniversary of the liberation of Auschwitz must be one of repentance and resolve to build a world where never again will such evil be possible. As Pope John Paul II said on the occasion of a concert last April commemorating the *Shoah:*

> We are gathered this evening to commemorate the Holocaust of millions of Jews. . . . We have a commitment, the only one perhaps that can give meaning to every tear . . . to ensure that evil does not prevail over good as it did for millions of children of the Jewish nation. (April 7, 1994)

This past year we rightly celebrated together the exchange of ambassadors between the Holy See and the state of Israel. But that celebration of light out of the darkness of the Holocaust we know was also on a deeper level a moral challenge. In the Fundamental Agreement of December 30, 1993, the Catholic Church and the Jewish people recommitted themselves to "cooperation in combating all forms of antisemitism and all kinds of racism and of religious intolerance, and in promoting mutual understanding among nations, tolerance among communities and respect for human life and dignity."

The half-century that has passed since the end of World War II should have taught us the dangers of turning away from violence, such as in the Balkans and Rwanda and widespread suffering within the human family. Global leadership on the part of the United States requires a consistent defense of human life, respect for human dignity, and generous assistance to those in desperate need.

The end of World War II brought dilemmas and opportunities for reordering global society. Today, fifty years later, the Cold War has ended and new possibilities for a better future beckon. In a statement anticipating the end of World War II, our predecessors as bishops of the United States offered a vision and a challenge that are as pertinent today as they were then:

> If the responsibility faced by the victors is great, the opportunity is historical. Now there comes the chance, not in hatred or vengeance but in justice and charity, to base a social reconstruction on truth and right. . . .
>
> The peoples of the world, the simple peoples, the fathers of families, the toilers and laborers, the people who have the same interests and the same ambitions which we cherish are looking to us, to this great land of freedom. We must not disappoint them. It is our historic opportunity to do our full duty in the family of nations. The causes of war must be removed, the honest needs of people must be met, their rights recognized. This must be a good peace which our victory will achieve. But let us first make ourselves in very truth peacemakers. Let us recognize the problems in our own social life and courageously seek the solution of them. A first principle must be the recognition of the sovereignty of God and of the moral law in our national life and in the right ordering of a new world born of the sacrifices and hardships of war. (Administrative Board, NCWC, in the name of the bishops of the United States, November 11, 1943)

Supported by One Root: Our Relationship to Judaism

Dutch Bishops
October 1995

For Christians, the Jewish religion has an essential and permanent meaning. This fundamental insight was formally articulated thirty years ago, on October 28, 1965, by the Second Vatican Council in the declaration *Nostra Aetate*. It showed that the Church cannot understand itself correctly when it ignores its relationship to Judaism.

Nostra Aetate stimulated a continuous development in the relationship between the Roman Catholic Church and Judaism. One of the ways in which this is expressed is in the Holy See's official recognition of the State of Israel and the establishment of reciprocal diplomatic relations. On that occasion the Roman Catholic Church expressly defined the obligation to combat every form of antisemitism.

Consistent with this development is the honest reflection on their own history that recently led the Polish and German bishops to recognize co-responsibility for the persecution of the Jews in the past. In all sincerity we join them in this sentiment.

SHOAH

In the same way that we are filled with gratitude this year when we recall the end of the War,[1] we are also filled with shame and dismay when we recall the

Shoah. Literally, this Hebrew word means "catastrophe." It has come to refer to the murder perpetrated on the Jewish people in those parts of Europe occupied by Germany in the years 1933 to 1945. From our country the second highest percentage of Jews was deported and murdered. This thought holds us in its grasp.

Looking back on the attitude of Dutch Catholics during the war, our thoughts turn to the courageous actions of the episcopacy then led by Archbishop J. de Jong. The occupiers punished this action by deporting and murdering Catholics of Jewish origin, among whom the Blessed Edith Stein. Others also witnessed in their resistance against the persecution of the Jews to authentic humanity and Christian faith.

ERRORS

But could Catholics not have done more? Were they not required to do more? These questions are too general to answer. The history of the twenty-century-long relationship between Jews and Christians is very complex and has left many traces of its passing. There is no doubt that church institutions have made errors.

A tradition of theological and ecclesiastical anti-Judaism contributed to the climate that made the *Shoah* possible. What was known as the "catechesis of vilification" taught that Jewry after Christ's death was rejected as a people.

Partly due to these traditions, Catholics in our country sometimes were reserved toward Jews, and sometimes indifferent or ill-disposed. Just after the war this was still apparent on the return of those who had been hidden from or who had survived the concentration camps.

We reject this tradition of ecclesiastical anti-Judaism and deeply regret its horrible results. With our pope and other episcopal conferences, we condemn every form of antisemitism as a sin against God and humanity.

CHANGE OF ATTITUDE

In the thirty years since *Nostra Aetate*, our Church has undergone a fortuitous change of attitude. A dialogue has been initiated between representatives of

Judaism and Christianity. In it Christians become more familiar with how Judaism sees itself, in its tradition and in its present situation, while Jews better understand who Jesus Christ is for us Christians. We rejoice in the results of this approach. But there is still much to do. Prejudice and forms of anti-semitism arise repeatedly in our society. This demands vigilance and decisiveness. Our Church has thus taken several initiatives.

In 1951 the Katholieke Raad voor Israel (Catholic Council for Israel) was established with the purpose of increasing awareness in our Church of the meaning of Judaism and improving our relationship. Last year we gave this council official status as an independent church institution.

In addition we inaugurated last year an episcopal commission for relations with Judaism which is intended to support the policy of the bishops' conference in this area. We appreciate the increased attention devoted to Judaism in Catholic theological education—not only in its historical meaning but also in its present form and the meaning it has now for the Christian tradition.

The dialogue between Christian Churches and Judaism has received a fixed form in The Netherlands in the Overlegorgaan van Joden en Christenen (Consultative Organization for Jews and Christians, OJEC). Via the Katholieke Raad voor Israel (Catholic Council for Israel), our Church participates in this organization.

VITALLY LINKED

Neither condemnation nor vilification, but respect and humility must determine our attitude to Judaism's role in God's history among people.

We Christians may never forget that Jesus of Nazareth is a son of the Jewish people, rooted in the tradition of Moses and the prophets. In meeting Judaism, we will better understand Jesus. In the scriptures, but also in our theology and liturgy, we remain vitally linked with the Jewish religion. Jews and Christians are sustained by the same root.

The more our actions are grounded in that awareness, the more we will contribute to the *shalom* promised to all peoples. We appeal to everyone to adopt the words Paul addressed to the Christians of Rome: "If the root is holy, so are the branches. But if some of the branches were broken off, and you, a wild olive shoot, were grafted in their place and have come to share the rich root of the olive tree, do not boast against the branches. If you do boast, consider that you do not support the root; the root supports you" (Rom 11:16-18).

Note

1. See *Liberated! Message from the Dutch Bishops on the Occasion of the 50 Years of Liberation* (May 1995) and *Message from the Dutch Bishops on the Commemoration of the Fiftieth Anniversary of the Independence of Indonesia* (July 1995). These documents can be obtained from the Secretariat for the Roman Catholic Church Community, box 13049, NL-3507 LA Utrecht, The Netherlands. Tel. + 31 30 233.42.44; fax. + 31 30 233.46.01; e-mail rcchinof@knoware.nl.

Confronting the Debate About the Role of Switzerland During the Second World War

Swiss Bishops' Conference
March 1997

The Bishops' Conference hereby contributes a study to the current debate in our country. The role of Switzerland during the Second World War has become the object of fierce debate. It is necessary to state that this role is appreciated very differently today by the generation that lived through and themselves remember the war years, than by the post-war generations whose approach is more historical. Confronted by this generational conflict, we are grateful to all those whose contributions serve to clarify the debate. Neither acts of injustice committed in the past nor the boundless suffering must sink into oblivion. It is necessary to extract a moral lesson with which to address the future so that such atrocities can never recur.

Our country, completely encircled by National Socialist and Fascist dictatorships, found itself in a precarious situation. Without complying with the totalitarian demands of her neighbors, Switzerland was nevertheless forced to make some compromises. In particular, Switzerland did not welcome as many refugees as she could have done so that the goods and fortunes of the victims and the persecuted could flow into Switzerland, permitting certain people to enrich themselves. We would like to evoke aspects of the past which reflect positively on our image. But we must also remind ourselves of the darker aspects of our history and accept the responsibility. We have inherited this past and have benefited from it. This enables us to be conscious of our obligations to make amends and to be ever vigilant in the face of the possibility of similar dangers, in the present or future, which now affects the manner in which we treat refugees or our responsibility with respect to acts of injustice.

At the time of Hitler's dictatorship and during the Second World War, unimaginable atrocities were committed, causing innumerable victims. The majority of these were the Jewish people, the designated target of the Holocaust. Indeed, this massacre was organized by a regime which also persecuted Christians and the churches. But we must not lose the perspective that, for centuries, Christians and ecclesiastical teachings were guilty of persecuting and marginalizing Jews, thus giving rise to antisemitic sentiments. Today, we shamefully declare that religious motivations, at that time, played a definite role in this process, motivations which are today largely incomprehensible. It is in reference to these past acts of churches for which we proclaim ourselves culpable and ask pardon of the descendants of the victims, as the Holy Father has done in preparation for the Year of Reconciliation (cf. *Tertio Millennio Adveniente*, nos. 33 and 36).

Being aware of our responsibility for the facts of our past, we consider it to be our obligation to affirm that Christianity has grown out of Judaism and that, consequently, the Christian faith is rooted in the Jewish tradition. In the face of National Socialist antisemitism, Pope Pius XI declared: "Through Christ and in Christ, we are the spiritual descendants of Abraham. Spiritually, we are all Semites" (cf. *La Documentation Catholique*, 1938, col. 1460). The Second Vatican Council emphasized that "the Jewish people still remain most dear to God because of their fathers, for he does not repent of the gifts he makes nor of the calls he issues. . . . His grace and his call are irrevocable. In company with the prophets and the same Apostle, the Church awaits that day, known to God alone, on which all people will address the Lord in a single voice. . ." *(Nostra Aetate,* no. 4). Their psalms are our prayers, through which we raise our concerns before God.

With the National Council of the Christian Churches, our position is to affirm that "antisemitism and the Christian faith are incompatible. The churches in Switzerland resolutely distance themselves from all antisemitic affirmations." We wish, through our Commission of Judeo-Roman Catholic Dialogue, to find the ways best suited to implant this consciousness better in the life of the Church.

Lessons To Learn from Catholic Rescuers

Cardinal William Keeler, U.S. Bishops
April 1997

I n 1990 the International Catholic-Jewish Liaison Committee began in newly liberated Prague, within a year of "the Velvet Revolution," a painful but necessary process of healing and reconciliation. This was a joint examination, country by country, of events that took place over a half-century ago that today we place together under the single, biblical term, *Shoah*.

Our joint examination of data and memory began with a visit to Theresienstadt—a major holding place for Jews being sent to the death camps, a place where many did in fact die because of disease and the wretched living conditions there, and, briefly, a "showpiece" used to deceive the Red Cross into believing that Jews were being treated humanely. Tragically, the world at large believed what it wanted to believe and did what it wanted to do, which was virtually nothing.

Today we celebrate the memory of some non-Jews—specifically Catholics—who did do something at a time of utmost crisis when most European Catholics either could not, or would not, help their neighbors in desperate need.

Our visit to Theresienstadt took place on a dark day, with a gentle rain falling, as if to underscore the sadness of our pilgrimage. When our group, emotionally drained, returned from Theresienstadt, Cardinal Edward I. Cassidy, president of the Pontifical Commission for Religious Relations with the Jewish People, rose to open the official meeting. What he said furnished a context for our reflections. The Church, he said, can only approach the *Shoah* in such a place and on such an occasion in a spirit of "repentance/*teshuvah*" for the evil that so many of its baptized members perpetrated and so many others failed to stop.

Similarly, when Pope John Paul II announced his plan for Christian preparation for the Jubilee Year 2000, he called on the Church first to examine its past failings and to acknowledge its need for repentance before God. This sense of repentance, of acknowledgment of the need for Catholic repentance, provides as well the proper context for our own celebration in the capital city of our own country. The saving deeds and lives of Catholics that we remember here today represent crucially important moral lights in a period of darkness. Our celebration of the brightness of that light and the preciousness of that witness is at once intensified and muted by the poignant awareness that they were, when all is said and done, relatively few among us, and no one can know how many, because some surely perished with those they tried to save.

The stories of the rescuers that we have heard here and read about elsewhere are truly remarkable. One such was Fr. Bernard Lichtenberg, rector of the Catholic cathedral in Berlin, who defied the German authorities Sunday after Sunday by preaching sermons against Nazism and condemning antisemitism and the persecution of Jews. He was picked up by the Gestapo, mistreated, and released. Heroically, he returned to the pulpit to continue his attacks on Nazi atrocities, was picked up again, and died on the way to Dachau. Last year Pope John Paul II, in a ceremony in Berlin, declared Bernard Lichtenberg blessed, which means a man whose virtuous life and heroic death by martyrdom make him worthy of veneration by all the world's Catholics—a model, that is, of proper attitude and behavior toward Jews and Judaism.

We have heard also of Polish[1] and Italian[2] nuns—representing those others all over Europe—who risked all to harbor thousands of Jews in their convents, even at the breach of cloister. Indeed, the story of Italy bears remembering. The Italians, although at first allied with and then occupied by the Nazis, saved over 80 percent of their Jewish neighbors, and the Italian Army saved thousands of others wherever it could reach them. Many of these stories have remained untold until very recently, and we remember here today those who have labored to preserve their memory—people like Rabbi Harold Schulweiss, Eva Fleischner, Sy Rotter and, of course, that most remarkable of Israeli institutions, Yad vaShem in Jerusalem.

We remember, too, Catholic groups such as the French Catholic resisters who, in opposition to both the Nazis and the collaborationist Vichy government, were led by such figures as Henri DeLubac (later to be named a cardinal) and who organized to save Jewish lives at the risk of their own.

We remember ZEGOTA, a distinctly and uniquely Polish organization, which risked all against unbelievable odds and whose story is told in the U.S. Holocaust Memorial Museum, Washington, D.C.

Shortly, we will hold a remembrance of the French Carmelite, Père Jacques Bunuel, on whom the museum has assembled a special exhibit.

It has been argued that to try to discern meaning in or to derive lessons from the Holocaust is fruitless at best and perhaps blasphemous. Can we, however, learn from the witness of the righteous? Surely, we who study the Holocaust need it, as Dr. Eva Fleischner has said: "We all need models of goodness if we are to believe in life."[3] And, just as surely, we Catholics who are teachers need such models if we are to be able to prepare the next generations of Christians properly for living moral lives in a world that can, as it did in the 1940s, descend into absolute moral chaos with dizzying rapidity.

If the righteous are to be our models for the future, we need to learn what the studies teach us about them. First, morality was deeply implanted in the fiber of their being, whether they were sophisticated and with advanced training or, as we would say in Maryland, "just folks." They frequently had to make a life-or-death decision on very short notice—perhaps a matter of minutes. Most of them say, in postwar interviews, that they felt they had little choice but to rescue. From their example we recognize the need for basic moral principles—what is right, what is wrong—to become deeply imbedded in our consciousness today, which is a lesson for public no less than private or religious education.

Second, the righteous had a deep sense that there was ultimate meaning to life beyond the present. While their understanding of that meaning may have varied, their experience reminds us of the need to place our lives in a wider context of human meaning and interrelatedness. We will hardly have the inner resources to respond to difficult moral challenges in our own day if we are only living for the present, if we are not open to the transcendent dimension with all that tells us about God and about our human pilgrimage through history. This underscores the critical importance of faith in God.

Third, many of the righteous had a prior acquaintance with Jews, though not necessarily with the people they actually rescued. From this we see the importance of building human bonds across religious, racial, and ethnic lines in times of relative social tranquillity. Otherwise, we will be in a poor position to try to establish those bonds in periods of social conflict and disruption.

Fourth, for us, as Catholics, the witness of the righteous challenges our identity as a church community. Dr. Helen Fein, writing in *Accounting for Genocide,* has argued that in the end many good people who faced difficult moral decisions under Nazi rule concluded that Jews could be regarded as "morally expendable." We, as Church, cannot allow that sort of calculation to persist any longer, whether for Jews or any other group of people.

As Pope John Paul II has insisted in his writings, particularly in his encyclicals *Redemptor Hominis* and *Evangelium Vitae,* authentic belief in Christ demands a firm commitment to human dignity for all persons. The righteous continue to remind us of the need to place the struggle for human rights at the very center of Christian consciousness.

In closing, I wish to express my gratitude to the U.S. Holocaust Memorial Museum, its chairman, Miles Lehrman, its executive director, Walter Reich, and its Subcommittee on Church Relations, for honoring the Catholic righteous this afternoon. My pledge to you in the name of the Catholic bishops and the other Catholics here assembled is that we as a Church will continue to combat antisemitism wherever, whenever, and in whatever form it may appear.

May God's special gifts of peace and health be with you all.

Notes

1. See Ewa Kurek, *Your Life Is Worth Mine: How Polish Nuns Saved Hundreds of Jewish Children in German-Occupied Poland, 1939-1945* (New York: Hippocrene Books, 1997).
2. See Margherita Marchione, *Yours Is a Precious Witness: Memoirs of Jews and Catholics in Wartime* (New York/Mahwah, N.J.: Paulist Press, 1997).
3. Eva Fleischner, "A Door That Opened and Never Closed: Teaching the *Shoah*," ibid, p. 28.

Declaration of Repentance

French Bishops
September 1997

A s one of the major events of the twentieth century, the planned extermination of the Jewish people by the Nazis raises particularly chal-
lenging questions of conscience which no human being can ignore.
The Catholic Church, far from wanting it to be forgotten, knows full well that
conscience is formed in remembering, and that, just as no individual person
can live in peace with himself, neither can society live in peace with a repressed
or untruthful memory.

The Church of France questions itself. It, like the other churches, has been
called to do so by Pope John Paul II as the third millennium draws near: "It is
good that the Church should cross this threshold fully conscious of what she
has lived through. . . . Recognizing the failings of yesteryear is an act of loyal-
ty and courage which helps us strengthen our faith, which makes us face up to
the temptations and difficulties of today and prepares us to confront them."[1]

Following this year's celebration of the fiftieth anniversary of the Declaration
of Seelisburg (that tiny village in Switzerland where, immediately after the war,
on August 5, 1947, Jews and Christians drew up guidelines proposing a new
understanding of Judaism), the undersigned bishops of France, because of the
presence of internment camps in their dioceses, on the occasion of the forth-
coming anniversary of the first statutes concerning the Jews drawn up by the
Maréchal Pétain government (October 3, 1940), wish to take a further step.
They do so in response to what their conscience, illuminated by Christ,
demands.

The time has come for the Church to submit her own history, especially that of this period, to critical examination and to recognize without hesitation the sins committed by members of the Church, and to beg forgiveness of God and humankind.

In France, the violent persecution did not begin immediately. But very soon, in the months that followed the 1940 defeat, antisemitism was sown at the state level, depriving French Jews of their rights and foreign Jews of their freedom. All of our national institutions were drawn into the application of these legal measures. By February 1941, some 40,000 Jews were in French internment camps. At this point, in a country which had been beaten, lay prostrate, and was partially occupied, the hierarchy saw the protection of its own faithful as its first priority, assuring as much as possible its own institutions. The absolute priority which was given to these objectives, in themselves legitimate, had the unhappy effect of casting a shadow over the biblical demand of respect for every human being created in the image of God.

This retreat into a narrow vision of the Church's mission was compounded by a lack of appreciation on the part of the hierarchy of the immense global tragedy which was being played out and which was a threat to Christianity's future. Yet many members of the Church and many non-Catholics yearned for the Church to speak out at a time of such spiritual confusion and to recall the message of Jesus Christ.

For the most part, those in authority in the Church, caught up in a loyalism and docility which went far beyond the obedience traditionally accorded civil authorities, remained stuck in conformity, prudence, and abstention. This was dictated in part by their fear of reprisals against the Church's activities and youth movements. They failed to realize that the Church, called at that moment to play the role of defender within a social body that was falling apart, did in fact have considerable power and influence, and that in the face of the silence of other institutions, its voice could have echoed loudly by taking a definitive stand against the irreparable.

It must be borne in mind: During the occupation no one knew the full extent of the Hitlerian genocide. While it is true that mention could be made of a great number of gestures of solidarity, we have to ask ourselves whether acts of charity and help are enough to fulfill the demands of justice and respect for the rights of the human person.

So it is that, given the antisemitic legislation enacted by the French government—beginning with the October 1940 law on Jews and that of June 1941, which deprived a whole sector of the French people of their rights as citizens, which hounded them out and treated them as inferior beings within the nation—and given the decision to put into internment camps foreign Jews who had thought they could rely on the right of asylum and hospitality in France, we are obliged to admit that the bishops of France made no public statements, thereby acquiescing by their silence in the flagrant violation of human rights and leaving the way open to a death-bearing chain of events.

We pass no judgment either on the consciences or on the people of that era; we are not ourselves guilty of what took place in the past; but we must be fully aware of the cost of such behavior and such actions. It is our Church, and we are obliged to acknowledge objectively today that ecclesiastical interests, understood in an overly restrictive sense, took priority over the demands of conscience—and we must ask ourselves why.

Over and above the historical circumstances which we already have recalled, we need to pay special attention to the religious reasons for this blindness. To what extent did secular antisemitism have an influence? Why is it, in the debates which we know took place, that the Church did not listen to the better claims of its members' voices? Before the war, Jacques Maritain, both in articles and in lectures, tried to open Christians up to a different perspective on the Jewish people. He also forcefully warned against the perversity of the antisemitism that was developing. Just before war broke out, Cardinal Saliege advised Catholics of the twentieth century to seek light in the teaching of Pius XI rather than in that of the thirteenth-century edicts of Innocent III. During the war, theologians and exegetes in Paris and in Lyons spoke out prophetically about the Jewish roots of Christianity, underlining how the shoot of Jesse flowered in Israel, that the two testaments were indissolubly linked, that the Virgin, Christ, and the apostles all were Jews, and that Christianity is linked to Judaism like a branch to the trunk that has borne it. Why was so little attention paid to such words?

Certainly, at a doctrinal level, the Church was fundamentally opposed to racism for the reasons, both theological and spiritual, which Pius XI expressed so strongly in his encyclical *Mit Brennender Sorge*, which condemned the basic principles of National Socialism and warned Christians against the myth of race and of the all-powerful state. As far back as 1928, the Holy Office had condemned antisemitism. In 1938, Pius XI boldly declared, "Spiritually, we are all Semites." But in the face of the constantly repeated anti-Jewish stereotypes, what weight could such condemnations carry? What weight could the thinking of theologians already referred to carry—thinking which can be found even after 1942 in statements which were not lacking in courage?

In the process which led to the *Shoah*, we are obliged to admit the role, indirect if not direct, played by commonly held anti-Jewish prejudices, which Christians were guilty of maintaining. In fact, in spite of (and to some extent because of) the Jewish roots of Christianity, and because of the Jewish people's fidelity throughout its history to the one God, the "original separation" dating back to the first century became a divorce, then an animosity, and ultimately a centuries-long hostility between Christians and Jews.

There can be no denying the weight of social, political, cultural, and economic factors in the long story of misunderstanding and often of antagonism between Jews and Christians. However, one of the essential points in the debate was of a religious nature. This is not to say that a direct cause-and-effect link can be drawn between these commonly held anti-Jewish feelings and the *Shoah*, because the Nazi plan to annihilate the Jewish people has its sources elsewhere.

In the judgment of historians, it is a well-proven fact that for centuries, up until Vatican Council II, an anti-Jewish tradition stamped its mark in differing ways on Christian doctrine and teaching, in theology, apologetics, preaching, and in the liturgy. It was on such ground that the venomous plant of hatred for the Jews was able to flourish. Hence, the heavy inheritance we still bear in our century, with all its consequences which are so difficult to wipe out. Hence our still open wounds.

To the extent that the pastors and those in authority in the Church let such a teaching of disdain develop for so long, along with an underlying basic religious culture among Christian communities which shaped and deformed people's attitudes, they bear a grave responsibility. Even if they condemned antisemitic theories as being pagan in origin, they did not enlighten people's minds as they ought because they failed to call into question these centuries-old ideas and attitudes. This had a soporific effect on people's consciences, reducing their capacity to resist when the full violence of National Socialist antisemitism rose up, the diabolical and ultimate expression of hatred of the Jews, based on the categories of race and blood, and which was explicitly directed to the physical annihilation of the Jewish people. As Pope John Paul II put it, "an unconditional extermination . . . undertaken with premeditation."

Subsequently, when the persecution became worse and the genocidal policy of the Third Reich was unleashed within France itself, shared by the Vichy government, which put its own police force at the disposition of the occupier, some brave bishops[2] raised their voices in a clarion call, in the name of human rights, against the rounding up of the Jewish population. These public statements, though few in number, were heard by many Christians.

Neither should the many actions undertaken by ecclesiastical authorities to save men, women, and children in danger of death be forgotten; nor the outpouring of Christian charity by the ordinary faithful, shown in generosity of every kind, often at great risk, in saving thousands and thousands of Jews.

Long before this, priests, religious, and lay people—some not hesitating to join underground movements—saved the honor of the Church, even if discreetly and anonymously. This also was done, in particular through the publication of *Les Cahiers du Témoignage Chrétien* (Notebooks of Christian Witness), by denouncing in no uncertain terms the Nazi poison which threatened Christian souls with all its neopagan, racist, and antisemitic virulence, and by echoing the words of Pius XI: "Spiritually, we are all Semites." It is an established historical fact that the survival of a great number of Jews was assured thanks to such gestures of help from among Catholic and Protestant milieux, and by Jewish organizations.

Nevertheless while it may be true that some Christians—priests, religious, and lay people—were not lacking in acts of courage in defense of fellow human beings, we must recognize that indifference won the day over indignation in the face of the persecution of the Jews and that, in particular, silence was the rule in face of the multifarious laws enacted by the Vichy government, whereas speaking out in favor of the victims was the exception.

As François Mauriac wrote, "A crime of such proportions falls for no small part on the shoulders of all those witnesses who failed to cry out, and this whatever the reason for their silence."[3]

The end result is that the attempt to exterminate the Jewish people, instead of being perceived as a central question in human and spiritual terms, remained a secondary consideration. In the face of so great and utter a tragedy, too many of the Church's pastors committed an offense, by their silence, against the Church itself and its mission.

Today we confess that such a silence was a sin. In so doing, we recognize that the Church of France failed in her mission as teacher of consciences and that therefore she carries along with the Christian people the responsibility for failing to lend their aid, from the very first moments, when protest and protection were still possible as well as necessary, even if, subsequently, a great many acts of courage were performed.

This is the fact that we acknowledge today. For this failing of the Church of France and of her responsibility toward the Jewish people are part of our history. We confess this sin. We beg God's pardon, and we call upon the Jewish people to hear our words of repentance.

This act of remembering calls us to an ever keener vigilance on behalf of humankind today and in the future.

Notes

1. John Paul II, *On the Coming of the Third Millennium (Tertio Millennio Adveniente)*, no. 33.
2. In 1942 five archbishops and bishops in the southern (unoccupied) part of France protested against the violation of human rights caused by the rounding up of the Jews. They were Archbishop Saliege of Toulouse; Bishop Theas of Montauban; Cardinal Gerlier of Lyons; Archbishop Moussaron of Albi; and Bishop Daly of Marseilles. Within the occupied zone, Bishop Vansteenberghe of Bayonne published a protest on the front page of his diocesan newsletter Sept. 20, 1942.
3. From the Preface to Leon Poliakov's book, *Bréviaire de la haine* (Breviary of Hate), 1951, p. 3.
   N.B.
   —The German bishops and the Polish bishops each published a declaration on the attitude of their churches during the war on the occasion of the fiftieth anniversary of the liberation of Auschwitz. [These statements appear in this volume, pp. 9-15.]
   —The legislation passed by the Vichy government, and particularly the Jewish statutes of 1940 and 1941, can be found in *Les Juifs sous l'Occupation. Recueil des*

textes officiels français et allemands, 1940-1944, published by the FFDJF (1982), as well as in Michael R. Marrus and Robert O. Paxton, *Vichy France and the Jews* (New York: Schocken Books, 1983).

—The main stances taken by Protestants can be found in *Spiritualité, Théologie et Résistance* (Presses Universitaires de Grenoble, 1987), pp. 151-182.

Letter to the
Jewish Community of Italy

Italian Bishops
March 1998

*(The Italian Bishops' statement came in the form of a letter delivered to
Prof. Elio Toaff, the chief rabbi of Rome, and Dr. Tullia Zevi,
the president of the Jewish Community of Italy.)*

We have come to this place (the Great Synagogue of Rome), representatives of the Secretariat for Ecumenism and Dialogue of the Episcopal Conference of Italy. We wish our presence here to be a sign of friendship and hope: of our friendship toward you our "elder brothers," firstborn in the faith who have so much to tell us of the centuries-old treasure of biblical tradition; and of the hope that the maleficent plant of antisemitism will be extinguished forever from history, beginning with our cultural and linguistic habits.

In these days, we remember that one hundred and fifty years ago civil liberty was given by Carlo Alberto to the Waldensians and the Jews in his kingdom. It is a joyous memory in which we participate. But we also remember that sixty years ago racial laws were enacted against the Jews in Italy. This is a most painful memory that questions and disquiets us. "Antisemitism has no justification and is absolutely condemnable," John Paul II repeated for all with firmness and clarity on November 1, 1997, in his speech to the participants of the Vatican Symposium on the Relationship Between the Christians and Jews.

38

From our common biblical font we are fond of remembering in this regard two imperatives frequently used: *shema*, listen, and *zechor*, remember; and one word without any equivocation, *teshuvah*, repentance.

It is true, as you have said, Rabbi Toaff, that "in Italy we had antisemitism of state not of the populace." But this does not take away from the fact that we deal with a dark page in the recent history of our country (the *Shoah*). Christian clergy for long centuries had cultivated "erroneous and unjust interpretations of scripture" (John Paul II, November 1, 1997). Because of this, we did not know how to muster energies capable of denouncing or to oppose with the necessary force and timeliness the iniquity that struck you.

However, spontaneous human charity and Christian solidarity with the Jewish people, and in particular of many priests and religious, did come to mitigate in some manner the lack of prophetic action when the situation passed from the violence of words to violence against persons. Yet such individual deeds were not sufficient to stop the catastrophe.

We recall these events with dismay and also with a profound and conscientious *teshuvah*. We do not want to, nor can we, forget the victims. We remember them to learn and to hearken even more to the Eternal who loves life, the one Lord of all who knows our thoughts and acts. We resolve to be open to the full biblical truth, beginning with the eminent dignity of humankind, upon which we reflected on this year's "Day of Solidarity with Judaism," January 17, 1998.

We recall with pleasure the initiative launched ten years ago by our secretariat to develop guidelines for the correct presentation of Judaism in preaching and catechesis. It has been received even on the European level. We proposed it in fact to the Ecumenical Assembly of Gratz last June before all the churches of Europe, achieving complete acceptance. On that occasion many were impressed by our firm position, as was stated of Professor René Samuel Sirat, chief rabbi of France, who was present. After unspeakable sufferings, truth has won over falsehood. Such a victory, however, is always fragile. It requires continual vigilance and permanent realization.

For its part, the Catholic Church, beginning with the Second Vatican Council—and thanks to the meeting of two men of faith, Jules Isaac and John

XXIII, whose memory is a blessing—decisively turned in another direction, removing every pseudotheological justification for the accusation of deicide and perfidy and also the theory of substitution with its consequent "teaching of contempt," the foundation for all antisemitism. The Church recognizes with St. Paul that the gifts of God are irrevocable and that even today Israel has a proper mission to fulfill: to witness to the absolute lordship of the Most High, before whom the heart of every person must open.

In our times, what does our past ask of us? To recognize the truth, however painful, of the facts and of our responsibility. The Catholic Church in Italy shows clearly that it does not intend to exempt itself from this duty in spite of the delay, and despite some incautious voices still lingering over prejudices that have been hard to die out.

We leave to the historians the task of doing their best to reconstruct the truth of facts still drenched with emotion. As for you, only the Eternal knows through what iniquity and inhuman tribulation you have passed, remaining heroically faithful to your vocation as witnesses to God's name. For us it is asked to accelerate the removal of prejudices and injustices and to encourage esteem and respect; opening the mind and heart to the fraternity that unites us in the love of the one Lord and Father. It is a path of purification of remembrance for which we ask trust and good will. We ask as well the pardon of the Lord who is "slow to anger and abounding in steadfast love" (Ps 103:8).

It is a sign of reconciliation that we want to share. We are called to bear witness together in this our time, still so discordant and lacerated, to collaborate in the defense of liberty and justice and to secure civil and religious rights for all, beginning with our own country and everywhere among all peoples.

With these sentiments we are here to render homage, dear chief rabbi and president, to you, to your associates, to the rabbis, and to the members of the Italian Jewish community. We hope that our more positive relationship in the renewed context of civil and religious liberty will lead us to cooperate for the good of all in the anticipation of the kingdom.

Part II:
1998 VATICAN
STATEMENT
AND
COMMENTARIES

Letter of Pope John Paul II

To my venerable brother, Cardinal Edward Idris Cassidy:

On numerous occasions during my pontificate I have recalled with a sense of deep sorrow the sufferings of the Jewish people during the Second World War. The crime which has become known as the *Shoah* remains an indelible stain on the history of the century that is coming to a close.

As we prepare for the beginning of the third millennium of Christianity, the Church is aware that the joy of a jubilee is above all the joy that is based on the forgiveness of sins and reconciliation with God and neighbor. Therefore she encourages her sons and daughters to purify their hearts through repentance of past errors and infidelities. She calls them to place themselves humbly before the Lord and examine themselves on the responsibility which they too have for the evils of our time.

It is my fervent hope that the document "We Remember: A Reflection on the *Shoah*," which the Commission for Religious Relations with the Jews has prepared under your direction, will indeed help to heal the wounds of past misunderstandings and injustices. May it enable memory to play its necessary part in the process of shaping a future in which the unspeakable iniquity of the *Shoah* will never again be possible. May the Lord of history guide the efforts of Catholics and Jews and all men and women of good will as they work together for a world of true respect for the life and dignity of every human being, for all have been created in the image and likeness of God.

March 12, 1998

Statement on Presenting the Document

Cardinal Edward Idris Cassidy
March 1998

T he Holy See has to date published, through its Commission for Religious Relations with the Jews, two significant documents intended for the application of the Second Vatican Council's declaration *Nostra Aetate*, no. 4: the 1974 *Guidelines and Suggestions,* and the 1985 *Notes on the Correct Way to Present the Jews and Judaism in Preaching and Catechesis in the Catholic Church.*

Today it publishes another document, which the Holy See's Commission for Religious Relations with the Jews has prepared at the express request of His Holiness Pope John Paul II. This document, which contains a reflection on the *Shoah,* is another step on the path marked out by the Second Vatican Council in our relations with the Jewish people. In the words which His Holiness wrote in his letter to me as president of the commission, it is our fervent hope "that the document . . . will help to heal the wounds of past misunderstandings and injustice."[1]

It is addressed to the Catholic faithful throughout the world, not only in Europe where the *Shoah* took place, hoping that all Christians will join their Catholic brothers and sisters in meditating on the catastrophe which befell the Jewish people, on its causes, and on the moral imperative to ensure that never again will such a tragedy happen. At the same time it asks our Jewish friends to hear us with an open heart.

On the occasion of a meeting in Rome on August 31, 1987, of representatives of the Holy See's Commission for Religious Relations with the Jews and of the International Jewish Committee on Interreligious Consultations, the then president of the Holy See's Commission for Religious Relations with the Jews, Cardinal Johannes Willebrands, announced the intention of the commission to prepare an official Catholic document on the *Shoah*. The following day, September 1, 1987, the participants in this meeting were received at Castel Gandolfo by His Holiness Pope John Paul II, who affirmed the importance of the proposed document for the Church and for the world. His Holiness spoke of his personal experience in his native country and his memories of living close to a Jewish community now destroyed. He recalled a recent address to the Jewish community in Warsaw, in which he spoke of the Jewish people as a *force of conscience* in the world today and of the Jewish memory of the *Shoah* as "a warning, a witness, and a silent cry" to all humanity. Citing the exodus of the Jewish people from Egypt as a paradigm and a continuing source of hope, His Holiness expressed his deep conviction that, with God's help, evil can be overcome in history, even the awesome evil of the *Shoah*.

We can read in the Joint Press Communiqué which was released at that time, that the Jewish delegation warmly welcomed the initiative of an official Catholic document on the *Shoah*, and expressed the conviction that such a document will contribute significantly to combating attempts to revise and to deny the reality of the *Shoah* and to trivialize its religious significance for Christians, Jews, and humanity.

In the years following the announcement, the Holy See's Commission for Religious Relations with the Jews engaged in a process of consciousness-raising and of reflection on several levels in the Catholic Church and in different places.

In the *Guidelines and Suggestions for Implementing the Conciliar Declaration Nostra Aetate, no. 4*, published on December 1, 1974, the Holy See's commission recalled that "the step taken by the Council finds its historical setting in circumstances deeply affected by the *memory* of the persecution and massacre of the Jews which took place in Europe just before and during the Second World War." Yet, as the *Guidelines* pointed out, "the problem of Jewish-Christian relations concerns the Church as such, since it is when 'pondering her own mystery' *(Nostra Aetate,* no. 4) that she encounters the mystery of

Israel. Therefore, even in areas where no Jewish communities exist, this remains an important problem."

Pope John Paul II himself has repeatedly called upon us to see where we stand with regard to our relations with the Jewish people. In doing so, "we must *remember* how much the balance [of these relations] over two thousand years has been negative."[2] This long period "which," in the words of Pope John Paul II, "we must not tire of reflecting upon in order to draw from it the appropriate lessons"[3] has been marked by many manifestations of anti-Judaism and antisemitism, and, in this century, by the horrifying events of the *Shoah*.

Therefore, the Catholic Church wants all Catholics, and indeed all people, everywhere, to know about this. It does so also with the hope that it will help Catholics and Jews towards the realization of those universal goals that are found in their common roots. In fact, whenever there has been guilt on the part of Christians, this burden should be a call to repentance. As His Holiness has put in on one occasion, "guilt must always be the point of departure for conversion."[4]

We are confident that all the Catholic faithful in every part of the world will be helped by this document to discover in their relationship with the Jewish people "the boldness of brotherhood."[5]

Notes

1. The letter of His Holiness is dated March 12, 1998.
2. Cf. Holy See's Commission for Religious Relations with the Jews, *Notes on the Correct Way to Present the Jews and Judaism in Preaching and Catechesis in the Catholic Church* (June 24, 1985).
3. John Paul II, speech delivered on the occasion of the visit to the synagogue of Rome, April 13, 1986. *Acta Apostolicae Sedis* 78 (1986): 1120, no. 4.
4. John Paul II, address to the ambassador of the new Federal Republic of Germany, November 8, 1990.
5. John Paul II, address to the diplomatic corps, January 15, 1994.

We Remember: A Reflection on the *Shoah*

Holy See's Commission for Religious Relations with the Jews
March 1998

I. TRAGEDY OF THE *SHOAH* AND THE DUTY OF REMEMBRANCE

The twentieth century is fast coming to a close, and a new millennium of the Christian era is about to dawn. The 2000th anniversary of the birth of Jesus Christ calls all Christians, and indeed invites all men and women, to seek to discern in the passage of history the signs of divine providence at work as well as the ways in which the image of the Creator in man has been offended and disfigured.

This reflection concerns one of the main areas in which Catholics can seriously take to heart the summons which Pope John Paul II has addressed to them in his apostolic letter *Tertio Millennio Adveniente*:

> It is appropriate that as the second millennium of Christianity draws to a close the Church should become more fully conscious of the sinfulness of her children, recalling all those times in history when they departed from the spirit of Christ and his Gospel and, instead of offering to the world the witness of a life inspired by the values of faith, indulged in ways of thinking and acting which were truly forms of counter-witness and scandal.[1]

This century has witnessed an unspeakable tragedy which can never be forgotten: the attempt by the Nazi regime to exterminate the Jewish people, with the consequent killing of millions of Jews. Women and men, old and young, children and infants, for the sole reason of their Jewish origin, were persecuted and deported. Some were killed immediately, while others were degraded, ill-treated, tortured, and utterly robbed of their human dignity, and then murdered. Very few of those who entered the camps survived, and those who did remained scarred for life. This was the *Shoah*. It is a major fact of the history of this century, a fact which still concerns us today.

Before this horrible genocide, which the leaders of nations and Jewish communities themselves found hard to believe at the very moment when it was being mercilessly put into effect, no one can remain indifferent, least of all the Church, by reason of her very close bonds of spiritual kinship with the Jewish people and her remembrance of the injustices of the past. The Church's relationship to the Jewish people is unlike the one she shares with any other religion.[2] However, it is not only a question of recalling the past. The common future of Jews and Christians demands that we remember, for "there is no future without memory."[3] History itself is *memoria futuri*.

In addressing this reflection to our brothers and sisters of the Catholic Church throughout the world, we ask all Christians to join us in meditating on the catastrophe which befell the Jewish people and on the moral imperative to ensure that never again will selfishness and hatred grow to the point of sowing such suffering and death.[4] Most especially we ask our Jewish friends, "whose terrible fate has become a symbol of the aberrations of which man is capable when he turns against God,"[5] to hear us with open hearts.

II. WHAT WE MUST REMEMBER

While bearing their unique witness to the Holy One of Israel and to the Torah, the Jewish people have suffered much at different times and in many places. But the *Shoah* was certainly the worst suffering of all. The inhumanity with which the Jews were persecuted and massacred during this century is beyond the capacity of words to convey. All this was done to them for the sole reason that they were Jews.

The very magnitude of the crime raises many questions. Historians, sociologists, political philosophers, psychologists, and theologians are all trying to learn more about the reality of the *Shoah* and its causes. Much scholarly study still remains to be done. But such an event cannot be fully measured by the ordinary criteria of historical research alone. It calls for a "moral and religious memory" and, particularly among Christians, a very serious reflection on what gave rise to it.

The fact that the *Shoah* took place in Europe, that is, in countries of long-standing Christian civilization, raises the question of the relation between the Nazi persecution and the attitudes down the centuries of Christians toward the Jews.

III. RELATIONS BETWEEN JEWS AND CHRISTIANS

The history of relations between Jews and Christians is a tormented one. His Holiness Pope John Paul II has recognized this fact in his repeated appeals to Catholics to see where we stand with regard to our relations with the Jewish people.[6] In effect, the balance of these relations over 2,000 years has been quite negative.[7]

At the dawn of Christianity, after the crucifixion of Jesus, there arose disputes between the early Church and the Jewish leaders and people who, in their devotion to the law, on occasion violently opposed the preachers of the Gospel and the first Christians. In the pagan Roman Empire, Jews were legally protected by the privileges granted by the emperor, and the authorities at first made no distinction between Jewish and Christian communities. Soon, however, Christians incurred the persecution of the state. Later, when the emperors themselves converted to Christianity, they at first continued to guarantee Jewish privileges. But Christian mobs who attacked pagan temples sometimes did the same to synagogues, not without being influenced by certain interpretations of the New Testament regarding the Jewish people as a whole.

"In the Christian world—I do not say on the part of the Church as such— erroneous and unjust interpretations of the New Testament regarding the Jewish people and their alleged culpability have circulated for too long, engendering feelings of hostility toward this people."[8] Such interpretations of the New Testament have been totally and definitively rejected by the Second Vatican Council.[9]

Despite the Christian preaching of love for all, even for one's enemies, the prevailing mentality down the centuries penalized minorities and those who were in any way "different." Sentiments of anti-Judaism in some Christian quarters and the gap which existed between the Church and the Jewish people led to a generalized discrimination, which ended at times in expulsions or attempts at forced conversions. In a large part of the "Christian" world, until the end of the eighteenth century those who were not Christian did not always enjoy a fully guaranteed juridical status. Despite that fact, Jews throughout Christendom held on to their religious traditions and communal customs. They were therefore looked upon with a certain suspicion and mistrust. In times of crisis such as famine, war, pestilence, or social tensions, the Jewish minority was sometimes taken as a scapegoat and became the victim of violence, looting, even massacres.

By the end of the eighteenth century and the beginning of the nineteenth century, Jews generally had achieved an equal standing with other citizens in most states and a certain number of them held influential positions in society. But in that same historical context, notably in the nineteenth century, a false and exacerbated nationalism took hold. In a climate of eventful social change, Jews were often accused of exercising an influence disproportionate to their numbers. Thus there began to spread in varying degrees throughout most of Europe an anti-Judaism that was essentially more sociological and political than religious.

At the same time, theories began to appear which denied the unity of the human race, affirming an original diversity of races. In the twentieth century, National Socialism in Germany used these ideas as a pseudoscientific basis for a distinction between so-called Nordic-Aryan races and supposedly inferior races. Furthermore, an extremist form of nationalism was heightened in Germany by the defeat of 1918 and the demanding conditions imposed by the victors, with the consequence that many saw in National Socialism a solution to their country's problems and cooperated politically with this movement.

The Church in Germany replied by condemning racism. The condemnation first appeared in the preaching of some of the clergy, in the public teaching of the Catholic bishops, and in the writings of lay Catholic journalists. Already in February and March 1931, Cardinal Bertram of Breslau, Cardinal Faulhaber and the bishops of Bavaria, the bishops of the province of Cologne, and those of the province of Freiburg published pastoral letters condemning National Socialism, with its idolatry of race and of the state.[10] The well-known Advent sermons of Cardinal Faulhaber in 1933, the very year in which National Socialism came to power, at which not just Catholics but also Protestants and Jews were present clearly expressed rejection of the Nazi antisemitic propaganda.[11] In the wake of the *Kristallnacht*, Bernhard Lichtenberg, provost of Berlin cathedral, offered public prayers for the Jews. He was later to die at Dachau and has been declared blessed.

Pope Pius XI too condemned Nazi racism in a solemn way in his encyclical letter *Mit Brennender Sorge*,[12] which was read in German churches on Passion Sunday 1937, a step which resulted in attacks and sanctions against members of the clergy. Addressing a group of Belgian pilgrims on September 6, 1938, Pius XI asserted: "Antisemitism is unacceptable. Spiritually, we are all Semites."[13] Pius XII, in his very first encyclical, *Summi Pontificatus*[14] of October 20, 1939, warned against theories which denied the unity of the human race and against the deification of the state, all of which he saw as leading to a real "hour of darkness."[15]

IV. NAZI ANTISEMITISM AND THE *SHOAH*

Thus we cannot ignore the difference which exists between *antisemitism*, based on theories contrary to the constant teaching of the Church on the unity of the human race and on the equal dignity of all races and peoples, and the long-standing sentiments of mistrust and hostility that we call *anti-Judaism*, of which, unfortunately, Christians also have been guilty.

The National Socialist ideology went even further, in the sense that it refused to acknowledge any transcendent reality as the source of life and the criterion of moral good. Consequently, a human group, and the state with which it was identified, arrogated to itself an absolute status and determined to remove the very existence of the Jewish people, a people called to witness to the one God and the law of the covenant. At the level of theological reflection we cannot ignore the fact that not a few in the Nazi Party not only showed aversion to the idea of divine providence at work in human affairs, but gave proof of a definite hatred directed at God himself. Logically such an attitude also led to a rejection of Christianity and a desire to see the Church destroyed or at least subjected to the interests of the Nazi state.

It was this extreme ideology which became the basis of the measures taken first to drive the Jews from their homes and then to exterminate them. The *Shoah* was the work of a thoroughly modern neopagan regime. Its antisemitism had its roots outside of Christianity, and in pursuing its aims, it did not hesitate to oppose the Church and persecute her members also.

But it may be asked whether the Nazi persecution of the Jews was not made easier by the anti-Jewish prejudices imbedded in some Christian minds and hearts. Did anti-Jewish sentiment among Christians make them less sensitive or even indifferent to the persecutions launched against the Jews by National Socialism when it reached power?

Any response to this question must take into account that we are dealing with the history of people's attitudes and ways of thinking, subject to multiple influences. Moreover, many people were altogether unaware of the "final solution" that was being put into effect against a whole people; others were afraid for themselves and those near to them; some took advantage of the situation; and still others were moved by envy. A response would need to be given case by case. To do this, however, it is necessary to know what precisely motivated people in a particular situation.

At first the leaders of the Third Reich sought to expel the Jews. Unfortunately, the governments of some western countries of Christian tradition, including some in North and South America, were more than hesitant to open their borders to the persecuted Jews. Although they could not foresee how far the Nazi hierarchs would go in their criminal intentions, the leaders of those nations were aware of the hardships and dangers to which Jews living in the territories of the Third Reich were exposed. The closing of borders to Jewish emigration in those circumstances, whether due to anti-Jewish hostility or suspicion, political cowardice, or shortsightedness, or national selfishness, lays a heavy burden of conscience on the authorities in question.

In the lands where the Nazis undertook mass deportations, the brutality which surrounded these forced movements of helpless people should have led to suspect the worst. Did Christians give every possible assistance to those being persecuted and in particular to the persecuted Jews?

Many did, but others did not. Those who did help to save Jewish lives, as much as was in their power, even to the point of placing their own lives in danger, must not be forgotten. During and after the war, Jewish communities and Jewish leaders expressed their thanks for all that had been done for them, including what Pope Pius XII did personally or through his representatives to save hundreds of thousands of Jewish lives.[16] Many Catholic bishops, priests, religious, and laity have been honored for this reason by the state of Israel.

Nevertheless, as Pope John Paul II has recognized, alongside such courageous men and women, the spiritual resistance and concrete action of other Christians was not that which might have been expected from Christ's followers. We cannot know how many Christians in countries occupied or ruled by the Nazi powers or their allies were horrified at the disappearance of their Jewish neighbors and yet were not strong enough to raise their voices in protest. For Christians, this heavy burden of conscience of their brothers and sisters during the Second World War must be a call to penitence.[17]

We deeply regret the errors and failures of those sons and daughters of the Church. We make our own what is said in the Second Vatican Council's declaration *Nostra Aetate,* which unequivocally affirms: "The Church ... mindful of her common patrimony with the Jews, and motivated by the gospel's spiritual love and by no political considerations, deplores the hatred, persecutions, and displays of antisemitism directed against the Jews at any time and from any source."[18]

We recall and abide by what Pope John Paul II, addressing the leaders of the Jewish community in Strasbourg in 1988, stated: "I repeat again with you the strongest condemnation of antisemitism and racism, which are opposed to the principles of Christianity."[19] The Catholic Church therefore repudiates every persecution against a people or human group anywhere, at any time. She absolutely condemns all forms of genocide as well as the racist ideologies which give rise to them. Looking back over this century, we are deeply saddened by the violence that has enveloped whole groups of peoples and nations. We recall in particular the massacre of the Armenians, the countless victims in Ukraine in the 1930s, the genocide of the Gypsies, which was also the result of racist ideas, and similar tragedies which have occurred in America, Africa, and the Balkans. Nor do we forget the millions of victims of totalitarian ideology in the Soviet Union, in China, Cambodia, and elsewhere. Nor can we forget the drama of the Middle East, the elements of which are well known. Even as we make this reflection, "many human beings are still their brothers' victims."[20]

V. LOOKING TOGETHER TO A COMMON FUTURE

Looking to the future of relations between Jews and Christians, in the first place we appeal to our Catholic brothers and sisters to renew the awareness of the Hebrew roots of their faith. We ask them to keep in mind that Jesus was a descendant of David; that the Virgin Mary and the apostles belonged to the Jewish people; that the Church draws sustenance from the root of that good olive tree on to which have been grafted the wild olive branches of the gentiles (cf. Rom 11:17-24); that the Jews are our dearly beloved brothers, indeed in a certain sense they are "our elder brothers."[21]

At the end of this millennium the Catholic Church desires to express her deep sorrow for the failures of her sons and daughters in every age. This is an act of repentance (*teshuvah*), since as members of the Church we are linked to the sins as well as the merits of all her children. The Church approaches with deep respect and great compassion the experience of extermination, the *Shoah* suffered by the Jewish people during World War II. It is not a matter of mere words, but indeed of binding commitment. "We would risk causing the victims of the most atrocious deaths to die again if we do not have an ardent desire for justice, if we do not commit ourselves to ensure that evil does not prevail over good as it did for millions of the children of the Jewish people. . . . Humanity cannot permit all that to happen again."[22]

We pray that our sorrow for the tragedy which the Jewish people has suffered in our century will lead to a new relationship with the Jewish people. We wish to turn awareness of past sins into a firm resolve to build a new future in which there will be no more anti-Judaism among Christians or anti-Christian sentiment among Jews, but rather a shared mutual respect as befits those who adore the one Creator and Lord and have a common father in faith, Abraham.

Finally, we invite all men and women of good will to reflect deeply on the significance of the *Shoah*. The victims from their graves and the survivors through the vivid testimony of what they have suffered have become a loud voice calling the attention of all of humanity. To remember this terrible experience is to become fully conscious of the salutary warning it entails: The spoiled seeds of anti-Judaism and antisemitism must never again be allowed to take root in any human heart.

March 16, 1998
Cardinal Edward Idris Cassidy, President
Bishop Pierre Duprey, Vice President
Rev. Remi Hoeckman, OP, Secretary

Notes

1. John Paul II, apostolic letter *Tertio Millennio Adveniente*. *Acta Apostolicae Sedis* (AAS) 87 (1995): 25, no. 33.
2. Cf. John Paul II, speech at the Rome synagogue, April 13, 1986. *AAS* 78 (1986): 1120, no. 4.
3. John Paul II, Angelus prayer, June 11, 1995. *Insegnamenti* 18/1 (1995): 1712.
4. Cf. John Paul II, address to Jewish leaders in Budapest, August 18, 1991. *Insegnamenti* 14/7 (1991): 349, no. 4.
5. John Paul II, encyclical *Centesimus Annus*. AAS 83 (1991): 814-815, no. 17.
6. Cf. John Paul II, address to episcopal conferences' delegates for Catholic-Jewish relations, March 6, 1982. *Insegnamenti* 5/1 (1982): 743-747.
7. Cf. Holy See's Commission for Religious Relations with the Jews, *Notes on the Correct Way to Present the Jews and Judaism in Preaching and Catechesis in the Roman Catholic Church*, June 24, 1985, VI, 1. *Enchiridion Vaticanum* 9, 1656.
8. Cf. John Paul II, speech to symposium on the roots of Anti-Judaism, October 31, 1997. *L'Osservatore Romano* (November 1, 1997): 6, no. 1.
9. Cf. Vatican Council II, *Nostra Aetate*, no. 4.
10. Cf. B. Statiewski, ed., *Akten Deutscher Bischöfe Über die Lage der Kirche, 1933-1945*, Vol. I, 1933-1934 (Mainz, 1968), Appendix.
11. Cf. L. Volk, *Der Bayerische Episkopat und der Nationalsozialismus 1930-1934* (Mainz, 1966), 170-174.
12. The encyclical is dated March 14, 1937. *AAS* 29 (1937): 145-167.
13. *La Documentation Catholique*, 29 (1938): col. 1460.
14. *AAS* 31 (1939): 413-453.
15. Ibid., 449.
16. The wisdom of Pope Pius XII's diplomacy was publicly acknowledged on a number of occasions by representative Jewish organizations and personalities. For example, on September 7, 1945, Dr. Joseph Nathan, who represented the Italian Hebrew Commission, stated: "Above all, we acknowledge the supreme pontiff and the religious men and women who, executing the directives of the Holy Father, rec-

ognized the persecuted as their brothers and, with efforts and abnegation, hastened to help us, disregarding the terrible dangers to which they were exposed" (*L'Osservatore Romano* [September 8, 1945]: 2). On September 21 of that same year, Pius XII received in audience Dr. A. Leo Kubowitzki, secretary general of the World Jewish Congress, who came to present "to the Holy Father, in the name of the Union of Israelitic Communities, warmest thanks for the efforts of the Catholic Church on behalf of Jews throughout Europe during the war" (*L'Osservatore Romano* [September 23, 1945]: 1). On Thursday, November 29, 1945, the pope met about eighty representatives of Jewish refugees from various concentration camps in Germany, who expressed "their great honor at being able to thank the Holy Father personally for his generosity toward those persecuted during the Nazi-Fascist period" (*L'Osservatore Romano* [November 30, 1945]: 1). In 1958, at the death of Pope Pius XII, Golda Meir sent an eloquent message: "We share in the grief of humanity. When fearful martyrdom came to our people, the voice of the pope was raised for its victims. The life of our times was enriched by a voice speaking out about great moral truths above the tumult of daily conflict. We mourn a great servant of peace."

17. Cf. John Paul II, address to the Federal German Republic's new ambassador to the Holy See, November 8, 1990. AAS 83 (1991): 587-588, no. 2.

18. *Nostra Aetate*, no. 4. Translation by Walter M. Abbott, SJ, in *The Documents of Vatican II.*

19. John Paul II, address to Jewish leaders in Strasbourg, October 9, 1988. *Insegnamenti* 11/3 (1988): 1134, no. 8.

20. John Paul II, address to the diplomatic corps, January 15, 1994. *AAS* 86 (1994): 816, no. 9.

21. John Paul II, Rome synagogue speech, no. 4.

22. John Paul II, address at a commemoration of the *Shoah*, April 7, 1994. *Insegnamenti* 17/1 (1994): 897 and 893, no. 3.

Implications of the Document on the Shoah

Cardinal William Keeler and Eugene Fisher
March 1998

American Catholics will welcome the statement on the Holocaust issued earlier today by the Holy See's Commission for Religious Relations with the Jews. Addressed to the universal Church, it will provide a significant resource and guide for us in the United States in our own ongoing efforts to grapple with the enormity of the evil of the *Shoah* and its implications for all Christians today.

The document directs us to contemplate what was done and was not done by Christians in those terrible years and over the centuries leading up to them. It properly expresses the Church's sense of repentance for the failures of that long and complex history. It presents us as well with the record of the righteous who did try to save Jews against all odds and at the risk of their lives.

This twin focus, repentance for the past and hope for the future, challenges Catholics in the United States in many ways. First, we must commit our resources, our historians, sociologists, theologians, and other scholars, as the document mandates, to study together with their Jewish counterparts all the evidence with a view to a healing of memories, a reconciliation of history.

Second, we must look at the implications of this document for our educational programs, its opportunities for rethinking old categories as well as probing the most difficult areas of moral thought. To take the Holocaust seriously is to look back at centuries of Christian misunderstandings both of Judaism and of the New Testament itself, as the text emphasizes, and seek to replace them with more accurate appreciations of both. How shall we embody what this statement calls us to do in our classrooms and from our pulpits?

However we answer these questions we will inevitably be moved to a more profound understanding of ourselves and of our future dialogue with the Jewish people.

Finally, in the short run, the statement will be a valuable resource in developing the themes of repentance and interreligious relations in the last year before the millennium/jubilee year. Pope John Paul II has called the twentieth century "the century of the *Shoah*." Sincere, contrite reflection and meditation on the Holocaust by Christians, especially in the presence of their Jewish neighbors, can embed our commemorations of the turning of the millennium in a realistic awareness of the nature of evil and impel us to stand together with the Jewish people to witness to one God, who calls to us.

A Step Forward in an Ongoing Dialogue

Cardinal John O'Connor
March 1998

I welcome the publication of "We Remember: A Reflection on the *Shoah*" as another development in the history of the Church's relationship with the Jewish people.

"We Remember: A Reflection on the *Shoah*" examines the failure of many in the Church in responding to the persecution and the suffering of the Jewish people during the Holocaust. While recognizing that the roots of Nazi anti-semitism grew outside the Church, it also addresses unambiguously and directly the erroneous and unjust application of church teaching on the part of many, which led, at least in part, to a climate which made it easier for the Nazis to carry out their Holocaust.

I know that some people of good will might find fault with this document, wishing it were "stronger," or that a certain word or phrase might have been used, or that the tone or substance of the document might have been different in some way. I can understand how some might feel that way.

It is my hope, however, that many people will read "We Remember: A Reflection on the *Shoah*" and see it as another step forward in the ongoing dialogue between Catholics and Jews. As the document says, "We pray that our sorrow for the tragedy which the Jewish people has suffered in our century will lead to a new relationship with the Jewish people. We wish to turn awareness of past sins into a firm resolve to build a new future in which there will be no more anti-Judaism among Christians or anti-Christian sentiment among Jews." This is my prayer as well.

Reflections Regarding the Vatican's Statement on the *Shoah*

Cardinal Edward Idris Cassidy
May 1998

THE DOCUMENT

I am pleased to have this opportunity of reflecting with you this morning on the document published by the Holy See's Commission for Religious Relations with the Jews on March 16 of this year entitled "We Remember: A Reflection on the *Shoah*." But before I begin that reflection I would like to pay tribute to the contribution which the American Jewish Committee has made and continues to make to the process of reconciliation between Catholics and the Jewish communities not only within the United States of America but throughout the world. Your friendship and understanding and cooperation are greatly appreciated by the commission that I head, the Commission for Religious Relations with the Jews. We look forward to continuing working with you in the years ahead so that we Jews and Christians may indeed, to use some words of Pope John Paul II, "be a blessing to each other" and in this way be a blessing for the world. I'm particularly appreciative of Rabbi Rudin's very sincere friendship, a friendship which I am most grateful for as are all the members of our Commission for Religious Relations with the Jews. You may not believe it but he sends me a letter every week and we thus are able to keep in touch with many of the things that are happening here in the United States in the Jewish world.

Our document is the result of a process of reflection that began with the preparations for the visit of Pope John Paul II to the United States in September 1987. This was an especially difficult time for Jewish-Catholic relations. During a meeting in Rome in the summer of that year between representatives of the Holy See's Commission for Religious Relations with the Jews and of the International Jewish Committee on Interreligious Consultations, my predecessor in the office of president of the Commission for Religious Relations with the Jews agreed that the commission would begin a study with the view of having a Vatican document on the relation of the Church to the *Shoah*. On the following day, September 1, 1987, the participants in this meeting were received at Castelgandolfo by Pope John Paul II, who affirmed the importance of the proposed document for the Church and for the world.

In the years following that decision, the Holy See's Commission for Religious Relations with the Jews engaged in a process of consciousness raising and of reflection on the *Shoah* at several levels in the Catholic Church, and in different local churches.

Work began on the document soon after I took over responsibility for the Holy See's commission in January 1990, and we set out with the idea that one single document would cover all that the Catholic Church throughout the world might wish to state on this great tragedy of the twentieth century.

As the work proceeded, it became clear, however, that the experience and involvement of the local churches throughout the world in relation to the *Shoah* were very different. What the Church in Germany or Poland would want to say in this regard would not be identical, and even their statements would not be appropriate for the particular churches in other continents.

The bishops' conferences in Germany, Poland, the Netherlands, Switzerland, Hungary, and France went ahead and each issued a statement that, while dealing with the same general topic, referred in a special way to the particular experience of the peoples in their countries. Italy followed by presenting last March 16 a formal letter to the Italian Jewish community strongly condemning antisemitism and deeply regretting the past treatment of Jews in Italy. The way was thus open to the Holy See to speak to, and on behalf of the universal Church.

It is important to keep this fact in mind as one reads the Vatican's statement. We address our reflection to "our brothers and sisters of the Catholic Church throughout the world," and "we ask all Christians to join us in meditating on the catastrophe which befell the Jewish people." And we conclude with an invitation to "all men and women of good will to reflect deeply on the significance of the *Shoah*," stating that "the victims from their graves and the survivors through the vivid testimony of what they have suffered, have become a loud voice calling the attention of all of humanity. To remember this terrible experience is to become fully conscious of the salutary warning it entails: The spoiled seeds of anti-Judaism and antisemitism must never again be allowed to take root in any human heart."

It is also important for an objective understanding of the document to keep in mind that our commission saw in this initiative the possibility of promoting among the Catholics in those countries that were far removed by geography and history from the scene of the *Shoah* an awareness of past injustices by Christians to the Jewish people and encourage their participation in the present efforts of the Holy See to promote throughout the Church "a new spirit in Jewish-Catholic relations: a spirit which emphasizes cooperation, mutual understanding, and reconciliation, good-will and common goals, to replace the past spirit of suspicion, resentment, and distrust."[1]

In the *Guidelines and Suggestions for Implementing the Conciliar Declaration Nostra Aetate, no. 4*, published on December 1, 1974, the Holy See's Commission for Religious Relations with the Jews recalled that "the step taken by the council finds its historical setting in circumstances deeply affected by the *memory* of the persecution and massacre of the Jews which took place in Europe just before and during the Second World War." Yet, as the *Guidelines* point out, "the problem of Jewish-Christian relations concerns the Church as such since it is when 'pondering her own mystery' that she encounters the mystery of Israel. Therefore, even in areas where no Jewish communities exist, this remains an important problem."

Such a document had by its very nature to attract the attention of and not alienate those to whom it was addressed. As I stated in my presentation of this document on March 16, it is to be seen as "another step on the path marked out by the Second Vatican Council in our relations with the Jewish people," and I expressed our fervent hope at that time "that it 'will help to heal the wounds of past misunderstandings and injustices' (Pope John Paul II)."[2]

WHAT THE DOCUMENT STATES

As we approach the close of one Christian millennium and the birth of a third Christian millennium, the Church has been called by Pope John Paul II, in his apostolic letter *Tertio Millennio Adveniente*, to "become more fully conscious of the sinfulness of her children, recalling those times in history when they departed from the spirit of Christ and his Gospel and, instead of offering to the world the witness of a life inspired by the values of faith, indulged in ways of thinking and acting which were truly forms of counterwitness and scandal."[3]

The document "We Remember: A Reflection on the *Shoah*" is to be read in this context. Indeed, it concerns one of the main areas in which Catholics should seriously take to heart the pope's summons. While no one can remain indifferent to the "unspeakable tragedy" of the attempt of the Nazi regime to exterminate the Jewish people, for the sole reason that they were Jews, the Church has a special obligation to reflect on this "horrible genocide," "by reason of her very close bonds of spiritual kinship with the Jewish people and her remembrance of the injustices of the past." Moreover, "the *Shoah* took place in Europe, that is, in countries of long-standing Christian civilization."

This, states the document, raises the question of the relation between the Nazi persecution and the attitudes down through the centuries of Christians toward Jews. In such a short document it was not possible to dwell at any length on the history of these relations, but the text admits clearly the prevalence over many centuries of anti-Judaism in the attitude of the Church towards the Jewish people. It acknowledges the "erroneous and unjust interpretations of the New Testament regarding the Jewish people and their alleged culpability," a "generalized discrimination" in their regard "which ended at times in expulsions or attempts at forced conversions," attitudes of suspicion and mistrust, while in times of crisis "such as famine, war, pestilence or social tensions, the Jewish minority was sometimes taken as a scapegoat and became the victim of violence, looting, even massacres."

While lamenting this anti-Judaism, the document makes a distinction between this and the antisemitism of the nineteenth and twentieth centuries, based on racism and extreme forms of nationalism, theories contrary to the constant teaching of the Church on the unity of the human race and on the equal dignity of all races and peoples. The antisemitism of the Nazis was the fruit of a thoroughly neopagan regime, with its roots outside of Christianity and, in pursuing its aims, it did not hesitate to oppose the Church and persecute its members also. The Nazi regime intended "to exterminate the Jewish people . . . for the sole reason of their Jewish origin."

No attempt is made in the document to deny that "the Jewish people have suffered much at different times and in many places while bearing their unique witness to the Holy One of Israel and to the Torah." "But the *Shoah* was certainly the worst suffering of all. The inhumanity with which the Jews were persecuted and massacred during this century is beyond the capacity of words to convey. *All this was done to them for the sole reason that they were Jews*" (my emphasis).

That does not mean of course that the Nazi persecution of the Jews was not made easier by the anti-Jewish prejudices imbedded in some Christian minds and hearts. This is clear in the document. What we state, however, is that before making accusations against people as a whole or individuals, one must know what precisely motivated them in a particular situation.

There were members of the Church who did everything in their power to save Jewish lives, even to the point of placing their own lives in danger. Many did not. Some were afraid for themselves and those near to them; some took advantage of the situation; and still others were moved by envy. Let me quote the document on this central point:

> As Pope John Paul II has recognized, alongside such courageous men and women (those who did their best to help), the spiritual resistance and concrete action of other Christians was not that which might have been expected from Christ's followers. We cannot know how many Christians in countries occupied by or ruled by the Nazi powers or their allies were horrified at the disappearance of their Jewish neighbors and yet not strong enough to raise their voices in protest. For Christians, this heavy burden of conscience of their brothers and sisters during the Second World War

must be a call to penitence. We deeply regret the errors and failures of those sons and daughters of the Church. . . .

At the end of this millennium the Catholic Church desires to express her deep sorrow for the failures of her sons and daughters in every age. This is an act of repentance (*teshuvah*), since, as members of the Church, we are linked to the sins as well as to the merits of all her children.

While remembering the past, the Vatican document looks to a new future in relations between Jews and Christians, reminding members of the Church of the Hebrew roots of their faith and that the Jews are their dearly beloved brothers, indeed in a certain sense their "elder brothers."[4]

"We Remember" closes with the prayer "that our sorrow for the tragedy which the Jewish people has suffered in our century will lead to a new relationship with the Jewish people. We wish to turn awareness of past sins into a firm resolve to build a new future in which there will be no more anti-Judaism among Christians or anti-Christian sentiment among Jews, but rather a shared mutual respect, as befits those who adore the one Creator and Lord and have a common father in faith, Abraham."

RELATION OF THIS DOCUMENT TO OTHER SIMILAR STATEMENTS

The document "We Remember: A Reflection on the *Shoah*" is not to be seen as the final word on all the questions raised in this reflection. While we do not foresee any other statement from the Vatican in the near future, I am sure that our document will result in renewed study and discussion. Indeed, this has been happening already with the publication of important articles by historians on Pope Pius XII and the Second World War. The document itself notes that "much scholarly study still remains to be done."

It is also important not to take the present document in isolation from those already issued by the episcopal conferences of several European countries or from the numerous statements made by Pope John Paul II in the course of his pontificate. There is no contradiction in these various texts. There is a variety in the tone and in the emphasis placed on certain aspects of the question, due as I have explained to the context in which they were issued and to the audience being addressed.

It is not possible this morning to dwell at any length on these other declarations, but I would like to look for a moment at the Drancy statement of the French bishops, issued on October 2, 1997 [see pp. 31-37 in this book]. This document received almost universal praise from Jewish circles.

The Drancy statement refers in particular to the period of the Vichy government, following the defeat of France by the German forces in 1940. While passing no judgment on the consciences of the people of that era nor accepting guilt for what took place at that time, the French bishops acknowledge that "too many of the Church's pastors committed an offense, by their silence, against the Church herself and her mission" in the face of the multifarious laws enacted by the government of that time.

The bishops find themselves "obliged to admit the role, indirect if not direct, in the process which led to the *Shoah* which was played by commonly held anti-Jewish prejudices, which Christians were guilty of maintaining." At the same time they state: "This is not to say that a direct cause-and-effect link can be drawn between these commonly held anti-Jewish feelings and the *Shoah*, because the Nazi plan to annihilate the Jewish people has its sources elsewhere."

REACTION TO THE DOCUMENT "WE REMEMBER: A REFLECTION ON THE *SHOAH*"

The publication of the Vatican document received an enormous amount of publicity worldwide. Our commission has been flooded with reactions from both Jewish and Catholic sources. I would like now to share with you an overall vision of these responses.

From the part of the Catholic Church—and it was to the members of this Church that the document was primarily addressed—the reactions have been very positive. This, as I have already indicated, is important, for the document was intended as one that would teach, arouse interest, and cause reflection within the worldwide Catholic community.

Many of the early comments from the Jewish community were instead distinctly negative. Such comments ranged from "Vatican document dismays Jews" *(Australian Jewish News);* "It is too late, after 53 years, and it's not enough" (Chief Rabbi Yisreal Lau of Israel); "Document skirts the issue of Church's long silences—Jewish reaction is cool" *(New York Times);* "An equivocal apology hurts more than it heals" *(Los Angeles Times);* to expressions of disappointment that this document was less forthright than those issued by various European bishops' conferences (Rabbi Leon Klenicki); that the apology contained therein was "less than unreserved" *(Melbourne Age);* and so on.

Other Jewish reactions were more positive. While not denying that they would have wished for a more definitive statement nor endorsing all the historical judgments contained in the document, these comments saw also positive aspects of the Vatican's statement: "*Mea culpa* is a good start" (Rabbi Raymond Apple, senior rabbi of the Great Synagogue Sydney); "The Vatican's welcome first step" (Dr. Paul Bartrop of Bialik College, Melbourne); "Jews didn't get everything they wanted, but what they got was so significant and it doesn't prejudice other important steps. The old things that gave rise to antisemitism are no longer part of Catholic doctrine" (Michael Berenbaum, president of the Survivors of the Shoah Visual History Foundation);[5] "It is my sense that the document, if read in the context of history, represents both a true act of Christian repentance and an act of *teshuvah*" (David Gordis, president of Hebrew College in Brookline, Mass.);[6] "This is a dramatic statement" (Rabbi Kopnick of Fort Wayne).

Rabbi Kopnick in his comments points out a fact that many overlooked, namely: "The Vatican didn't have to do anything." Indeed, Sir Owen Chadwick, a British authority on the Vatican in the Second World War, in an article published in *The Tablet* on March 28, 1998, expresses the conviction that it would have been better to say nothing:

> The Holocaust is the most brutal thing that ever happened. There are still people who suffer from it. There are still people living who remember fathers or brothers or sisters who died in some camp in eastern Europe though they were innocent of wrong. Nothing that anyone could ever say in the way of apology or sorrow or repentance can ever be adequate; anything that is said is bound to be

resented. If you wish to avoid resentment (which is a good thing to avoid), say nothing.

I cannot agree with this and was comforted by the reception given to the document in an editorial in *The Philadelphia Inquirer*, which received our document with this comment:

> The document released Monday by the Vatican, "We Remember: Reflection on the *Shoah*," is a remarkable, perplexing text, at once an acknowledgment, an apology, and a repentance. The very title is a breakthrough. How crucial that the Roman Catholic Church would tell the world "We remember the Holocaust": That puts an end to three generations of official silence.

Judith Banki, program director of the Marc Tanenbaum Center for Interreligious Understanding, in a letter to the *New York Times*, indicates another aspect of our document that has been generally overlooked. In my presentation to the press March 16, I pointed out that the Jewish delegation at the September 1, 1987, meeting with Pope John Paul II in Castel Gandolfo expressed the conviction that a Vatican document on the *Shoah* "will contribute significantly to combating attempts to revise and deny the reality of the *Shoah* and to trivialize its religious significance for Christians, Jews, and humanity." Judith Banki rightly, I believe, states that the document "We Remember: A Reflection on the *Shoah*" "stands as a clear rebuttal to an entire industry of Holocaust denial and revision. To some 800 million Catholic faithful and to the world at large, the Church has said 'it happened.' One cannot explain away as of no significance a document of the Catholic Church, inadequate or not in the opinion of the Jewish community, which expresses repentance for the actions or silence of its members in regard to a tragedy of 50 odd years ago. That tragedy must have happened."

SOME QUESTIONS RAISED IN THE DOCUMENT

One of the criticisms of the document we are reflecting upon is that it asks several important questions, but does not give a satisfactory reply to them. I would like to say a few words about three of these questions.

The first is "the relations between the Nazi persecution of the Jews and the attitudes down through the centuries of Christians toward Jews." It seems to me that it is particularly on this point that most disappointment has been expressed by Jewish leaders.

There can be no denial of the fact that from the time of Emperor Constantine on, Jews were isolated and discriminated against in the Christian world. There were expulsions and forced conversions. Literature propagated stereotypes; preaching accused the Jews of every age of deicide; the ghetto which came into being in 1555 with a papal bull, became in Nazi Germany the antechamber of the extermination.

It is also true that the Nazis made use of this sad history in their attacks on the Jewish people, adopting symbols and recalling events of the past to justify their deadly campaign. It is also true, I believe, that a part of the indifference shown toward the mass deportations and brutality which accompanied these forced movements of helpless and innocent people was a result of the age-old attitudes of Christian society and preaching toward those considered responsible for the death of Jesus.

But to make a jump from the anti-Judaism of the Church to the antisemitism of the Nazis is to misread the nature of the Nazi persecution. To quote from the Vatican document: "The *Shoah* was the work of a thoroughly modern neopagan regime. Its antisemitism had its roots outside of Christianity and, in pursuing its aims, it did not hesitate to oppose the Church and persecute her members also."

The Church can justly be accused of not showing to the Jewish people, down through the centuries that love which its founder, Jesus Christ, made the fundamental principle of his teaching. Rather, an anti-Jewish tradition stamped its mark in different ways on Christian doctrine and teaching. "To the extent that the pastors and those in authority in the Church let such teaching of disdain develop so long, and that they maintained among Christian communities an underlying basic religious culture which shaped and deformed peoples' attitudes, they bear a heavy responsibility. . . . This is not to say [however] that a direct cause-and-effect link can be drawn between these commonly held anti-Jewish feelings and the *Shoah*, because the Nazi plan to annihilate the

Jewish people had its sources elsewhere" (Drancy statement). At no time did the church authorities seek to exterminate the Jewish people!

A second question that perhaps needs some explanation is a distinction that the Vatican document makes between "the Church" and the "members of the Church." In our document we quote Pope John Paul II, who stated in an address to the October 1997 Vatican symposium on "The Christian roots of Anti-Judaism":

> In the Christian world—I do not say on the part of the Church as such—erroneous and unjust interpretations of the New Testament regarding the Jewish people and their alleged culpability have circulated for too long, engendering feelings of hostility toward this people.[7]

This distinction—the Church and the members of the Church—runs through the Vatican document and is not readily understood by those who are not members of the Catholic Church. Let me state firstly that when we make this distinction, the term "members of the Church" does not refer to a particular category of church members, but can include according to the circumstances popes, cardinals, bishops, priests, and laity.

For Catholics, the Church is not just the members that belong to it. It is looked upon as the bride of Christ, the heavenly Jerusalem, holy and sinless. We do not speak of the Church as sinful, but of the members of the Church as sinful—a distinction you may find hard to understand, but one which is essential to our understanding of the Church.[8] An editorial in the *Philadelphia Inquirer* on March 18, 1998, acknowledged that "in Catholic belief, it's impossible to conceive of the Church, divinely ordained and inspired, itself falling into such evil error. But through free will, individual Catholics, even very prominent ones, could so sin."

And that brings me to the third question raised by the Vatican document: the responsibility of certain individual members of the Church, holding the highest positions of responsibility. We have been criticized for mentioning by name some who spoke out against the Nazi ideology and antisemitism. The references to Pius XII, in particular, have been the object of much comment.

I think it important to give credit where credit is due. History will surely find guilty those who could have acted and did not, those who should have spoken and did not. We did not have the information that would have allowed us to enter into judgment of individuals who might have fallen within these categories.

As for Pope Pius XII, it is our conviction that in recent years his memory has been unjustly denigrated. You will all have read Kenneth Woodward's concise article "In Defense of Pius XII" in *Newsweek* of March 30. Why did we wish to bring Pius XII into our document? For the very reason that Kenneth Woodward wrote his article. Ever since the play of Rolf Hochhuth in 1963 "The Deputy," monstrous calumnies regarding Pius XII and the period of the Second World War have gradually become accepted facts, especially within the Jewish community. In one page, Woodward shows how unjust this process has been.

Already two important articles by historians have appeared supporting the claims made in the document "We Remember." One by Rev. Pierre Blet, SJ, published in *La Civiltà Cattolica* on March 21 and reproduced in *L'Osservatore Romano* on March 27. Father Blet is one of those who has studied all the documents in the Vatican Archives for the period of the Second World War. The second is an article in German, "Gerechtigkeit für Papst Pius XII," by Professor Herbert Scambeck of the Johannes Kepler University of Linz, Austria, published recently in the *Rheinischer Merkur*.

LOOKING TO A COMMON FUTURE

"We Remember" calls on Catholics to renew the awareness of the Hebrew roots of their faith. It expresses deep sorrow for the failures of the sons and daughters of the Church and states, "This is an act of repentance (*teshuvah*)." The Church approaches with deep respect and great compassion the experience of extermination, the *Shoah*, suffered by the Jewish people during World War II" and sees this as a binding commitment to ensure that "evil does not prevail over good as it did for millions of the children of Jewish people. . . . Humanity cannot permit all that to happen again." "Most especially," we read in the Vatican document, "we ask our Jewish friends 'whose terrible fate has become a symbol of the aberrations of which man is capable when he turns against God,' to hear us with open hearts."

Finally, we pray that our sorrow for the tragedy of the *Shoah* will lead to a new relationship between Catholics and Jews. Indeed we see this document as one step in the building up of that relationship.

I am well aware that declarations are not enough; the coming Christian jubilee calls for a real conversion, both internal and external, before God and before our neighbor. As members of the Church, but also as ordinary members of the human race, past history questions us. The silences, prejudices, persecutions, and compromises of past centuries weigh upon us. Is it possible for us, as human beings and as Christians, to kneel before God in the presence of the victims of all times to ask pardon and to hope for reconciliation? I believe that it is. And if it is possible, then we should do it without waiting or losing any time. Tomorrow may be too late. If we could heal the wounds that bedevil Christian-Jewish relations, we would contribute to the healing of the wounds of the world, the *tiqqun 'olam* (the mending of the world), which the Talmud considers to be a necessary action in building a just world and preparing for the kingdom of the most high.

Our recent document appeals not only to Catholics, but to all men and women of good will to make this kind of reflection, and I would see a particular challenge there for those Christians—Catholics, Orthodox, and Protestant—who seek to journey together along the ecumenical way of unity. Could they not join together in this act of *teshuvah*?

In his article published in *The Jewish Advocate* and already referred to above, David Gordis expressed the hope that Jews will see the document "We Remember" as a true act of Christian repentance and an act of *teshuvah*. He makes a comment that seems to me worthy of reflection when he writes:

> We have no "repentance" in Judaism; we have *teshuvah* or "return." The difference is important. As Jews reflect on the past, we look to a positive reshaping of our behavior and our relationship with God and with our fellow human beings. It is inevitable that we have missed the mark in small ways and big ways. We are called on not to punish ourselves, but to reshape our lives, to refocus ourselves to the good and proper way, to the path of God.

And he then goes on to quote Pope John Paul II's letter accompanying the Vatican document on the *Shoah,* in which the fervent hope is expressed that this document will help heal the wound of the past and "enable memory to play its necessary part in the process of shaping a future in which the unspeakable iniquity of the *Shoah* will never again be possible." David Gordis himself then expresses the hope that the document will be read in this way and that Jews will "welcome it as another step in making the world a better place, safer and more secure for all people."

This, I believe, is the challenge that faces us, Jews and Christians, in the face of growing secularism, religious apathy, and moral confusion, a place in which there is little room for God. We may feel secure in a pluralistic, liberal-orientated society, and there are good reasons to do so. Yet it might be wise to keep in mind the possibility that a society with little room for God may one day have little room for those who believe in God and wish to live according to his law and commandments.[9] Whenever we can give united witness to our common values, we should do so.

In any case, I am convinced that Christians and Jews have today a new opportunity of contributing together to the well-being of the societies of which we are both members and indeed to the world in which we live. The possibilities are immense: the care and conservation of the environment; respect for life; the defense of the weak and oppressed; the place of women in society; the promotion of the family; the protection of children; opposition to all forms of racism and antisemitism (which can also take the form of anti-Zionism); the education of future generations; and so on.

On the theme of the family, the International Catholic-Jewish Liaison Commission, during its 1994 meeting in Jerusalem, issued a joint statement on the importance of the family in society.[10] And the recent meeting of the commission which was held in Vatican City in March issued a similar document on the environment.[11]

Besides the diverse possibilities of cooperation in the field of human rights, there are challenges for us to work together for the protection of the rights of religion, for dialogue with the other great religions of the world—with a special place in this context for dialogue with the believing followers of Islam—and for collaboration in the realm of culture.

This calls for "cooperation, mutual respect and understanding, good will, and common goals," to quote once again the Prague 1990 statement of the International Catholic-Jewish Liaison Committee.[12] Jews and Christians must learn to listen to each other, to seek to understand the other as the other understands him/herself rather than approach the other with an attitude of criticism or wish to argue or enter into a debate, be open to and respect the other, work together without compromising their own faith or distinct identity, be seen as children of the one and only God who know that God loves them and wants all men and women to know and experience that love, to be together a "light to the nations."

With the document "We Remember: A Reflection or the *Shoah*," the Catholic Church has renewed its "binding commitment to ensure that evil does not prevail over good." We ask the Jewish community to take our hand and join us in this challenge.

Notes

1. Final Statement of the Prague 1990 meeting of the International Catholic-Jewish Liaison Committee (ILC). *Information Service of the Pontifical Council for Promoting Christian Unity 75* (1990): 176.
2. Letter of John Paul II to Cardinal Cassidy on the occasion of the publication of "We Remember: A Reflection on the *Shoah*." [This letter is printed in this volume, p. 43.]
3. John Paul II, apostolic letter *Tertio Millennio Adveniente*, November 10, 1994. AAS 87 (1995): 25, no. 33.
4. Pope John Paul II, speech at the synagogue of Rome, April 13, 1986. *AAS* (1986): 1120, no. 4.
5. Quoted in an editorial of *The Philadelphia Inquirer*, March 18, 1998.
6. *The Jewish Advocate*, April 3-April 9, 1998.
7. *L'Osservatore Romano* (November 1, 1997): 6.
8. No. 8 of the Second Vatican Council's dogmatic constitution *Lumen Gentium* distinguishes "the society furnished with hierarchical agencies and the Mystical Body of Christ" and states that they are not to be considered as two realities. "Rather they form one interlocked reality which is comprised of a divine and a human element." This reality is compared by the council to the mystery of the Incarnate Word.
9. In the former East Germany, less than 25 percent of the population has a church affiliation. The area known as "Lutherland" (Sachsen-Anhalt, which includes names dear to Lutherans, such as Wittenberg, Eisleben, etc.) was 90 percent Christian before the war. Only 7 percent today are Lutheran, 3 percent Catholic. There are a few Jews and Muslims. The rest are without a religion.

10. Fifteenth ILC Meeting, Jerusalem 1994, Final Statement.
11. Sixteenth ILC Meeting, Vatican 1998, Final Statement.
12. *Information Service* 75 (1990): 176.

Bibliography on Jewish-Christian Relations

Bernardin, Joseph. *A Blessing to Each Other: Cardinal Joseph Bernardin and Jewish-Catholic Dialogue* (Chicago: Liturgy Training Publications, 1996). Addresses and reflections of the late cardinal on the dialogue.

Cernera, Anthony J., ed. *Toward Greater Understanding: Essays in Honor of John Cardinal O'Connor* (Fairfield, Conn.: Sacred Heart University, 1995). Includes essays by Cardinals Bernardin, Cassidy, Keeler, and Law; by Rabbis Jack Bemporad, David Novak, Mordecai Waxman, and Walter Wurtzburger; and by Elie Wiesel.

Croner, Helga, ed. *Stepping Stones to Further Jewish Christian Relations* (New York: Stimulus Books, 1977); *More Stepping Stones* (New York: Paulist Press, 1985). These two volumes contain the statements of Protestant and Catholic Church bodies on Christian-Jewish relations.

Efroymson, David, Eugene J. Fisher, and Leon Klenicki, eds. *Within Context: Essays On Jews and Judaism in the New Testament* (Collegeville, Minn.: Liturgical Press, 1993). Roman Catholic scholars provide background on the New Testament with sensitivity to its Jewish milieu.

Fisher, Eugene J. *Faith Without Prejudice*, 2nd ed. (New York: Crossroad, 1993). A general introduction to the issues, with activities for parishes and schools and a selection of key Catholic documents.

Fisher, Eugene J., ed. *Interwoven Destinies* (New York: Paulist Press, 1993) and *Visions of the Other* (New York: Paulist Press, 1994). Six Christian and six

Jewish scholars are paired in looking at the history and contemporary possibilities of two millennia of Jewish-Christian interrelations.

Fisher, Eugene J. and Leon Klenicki. *In Our Time: The Flowering of Jewish-
Catholic Dialogue* (New York: Paulist Press/New York: Stimulus, 1990). Key
documents and commentary of the dialogue. Fifty-page annotated bibliog-
raphy-essay on the literature in the field.

―――. *From Desolation to Hope: An Interreligious Holocaust Memorial Service*
(Chicago: Liturgy Training Publications, 1990).

Fisher, Eugene J. and Leon Klenicki, eds. *Spiritual Pilgrimage: Pope John Paul II
on Jews and Judaism, 1979-1995* (New York: Crossroad, 1995). The pope's
statements, with introduction and thematic commentary by the editors.

Fisher, Eugene J. and James Rudin, eds. *Twenty Years of Jewish-Catholic Relations*
(New York: Paulist Press, 1986). Essays by leading figures in the American
dialogue since Vatican II on the council, liturgy, Israel, education, and the
Shoah.

Flannery, Edward J. *The Anguish of the Jews: Twenty-Three Centuries of
Antisemitism* (New York: Paulist Press, 1985). A historical survey of
Christian antisemitism by a noted Catholic author.

Gager, John G. *The Origins of Anti-Semitism* (New York: Oxford University
Press, 1983). Study of patristic literature.

Hertzberg, Arthur. *The French Enlightenment and the Jews* (New York: Columbia
University Press, 1968). Classic text revealing that in some ways the "en-
lightened" thinkers held darker and more racist views of Jews and Judaism
than their medieval or Reformation predecessors.

International Catholic-Jewish Liaison Committee. *Fifteen Years of Catholic-
Jewish Dialogue, 1970-1985* (Rome: Libreria Editrice Lateranense and
Libreria Editrice Vaticana, 1988).

Jacobs, Steven J., ed. *The Holocaust Now: Contemporary Christian and Jewish
Thought* (East Rockaway, N.Y.: Cummings & Hathaway, 1996). Twenty-two
scholars reflect on the *Shoah* and its implications for Jewish and Christian
theology.

Littell, Marcia and Sharon Gutman, eds. *Liturgies on the Holocaust: An Interfaith Anthology* (Valley Forge, Penn.: Trinity Press International, 1996).

Oberman, Heiko. *The Roots of Anti-Semitism in the Age of Renaissance and Reformation* (Philadelphia: Fortress, 1984). Erasmus, Reuchlin, Pfefferkorn, Calvin, Luther, and others.

Pawlikowski, John and James Wilde. *When Catholics Speak About Jews* (Chicago: Liturgy Training Program, 1987). Identifies difficulties in the lectionary and offers practical advice on how preachers can proclaim the Gospel free of a negative portrait of Jews and Judaism.

Saperstein, Marc. *Moments of Crisis in Jewish-Christian Relations* (Philadelphia: Trinity Press International, 1989). Concise survey of the history of Jews and Christians in antiquity, the Middle Ages, the Reformation, and during the Holocaust.

"SIDIC" is a journal published three times a year by the Sisters of Sion in Rome. It specializes in materials and articles on Jewish-Christian relations. It is available through the Secretariat for Ecumenical and Interreligious Affairs, National Conference of Catholic Bishops, 3211 Fourth St., NE, Washington, DC 20017.

Spiro, J. and H. Hirsch, eds. *Persistent Prejudice* (Fairfax, Va.: George Mason University Press, 1988). Essays on the history of antisemitism.

Synan, Edward A. *The Popes and the Jews in the Middle Ages* (New York: Macmillan, 1965). Relevant church texts and their historical contexts.

The Theology of the Churches and the Jewish People: Statements of the World Council of Churches and Its Member Churches (Geneva: WCC Publications, 1988). Includes commentaries by Alan Brockway, Paul van Buren, Rolf Rentdorff, and Simon Schoon.

Wilken, Robert L. *John Chrysostom and the Jews: Rhetoric and Reality in the Late Fourth Century* (Berkeley: University of California Press, 1983). Analyzes the anti-Jewish diatribes of a church father in historical context.

Willebrands, Cardinal Johannes. *Church and Jewish People: New Considerations* (New York: Paulist Press, 1992). Collects the texts and addresses of the head of the Holy See's Commission for Religious Relations with the Jews from 1974 to 1990.

Wolf, Alfred and Royale Vadakin, eds. *A Journey of Discovery: A Resource Manual for Jewish-Catholic Dialogue* (Valencia, Calif.: Tabor Publications, 1989). Handy, looseleaf format includes joint statements and resources developed by the Los Angeles Respect Life, Priest/Rabbi, and Women's Dialogue groups over the course of two decades. A valuable resource.